Can America Survive Its Future?

Dick, John, Tom,

Here is my last will and testament.

Ken

Can America Survive Its Future?

Kenneth R. Libbey

MacLean and Clark, Publishers
Decatur, Georgia

Can America Survive Its Future?

Cover design by Steve Libbey

MacLean and Clark, Publishers

1285 Vista Leaf Drive
Decatur, GA 30033
404-636-5728

The author may be contacted at
kenlibbey@comcast.net

ISBN: 0-9662206-4-1

Printed in the United States of America

This book is dedicated
to the young people who are struggling with a less forgiving society and a less promising future.

Contents

Preface

A little over 500 years ago, Christopher Columbus landed on a Caribbean island and has ever since been credited with discovering America. A little over 400 years ago, European colonists began populating the eastern coast of the new continent. A little over 200 years ago, the colonists had won their independence and begun an unrelenting push westward.

The America that Columbus "discovered" was actually the homeland of several million people, some nomadic but most living in villages and cities. As late as 1789, the third largest city in America, after Boston and Philadelphia, was a native city in the Mississippi Valley. The native Americans were connected by remarkably long-distance trading relationships and in some areas by durable federations or political hierarchies. They supported themselves by farming, fishing, hunting, and gathering, all of which they did with great knowledge of and respect for the natural resources on which they depended. They gave expression to this dependence in their religious beliefs and observances. They passed their traditions down through many generations.

By the time Europeans arrived, North America had supported human communities for over 12,000 years. In the 400 years of European occupation, the population has soared past 300 million, much of the natural habitat has been cleared or drained, and the per capita use of natural resources has reached a pace unrivaled anywhere in the world. We modern Americans have a relatively short history and we take a short-term view of life. The United States is in only its third century. Can it sustain its standard of living and way of life into a fourth century?

In 2000, during a long camping trip, I visited the site of the Yukon gold rush near Dawson City. I might as well have been on the moon. Everywhere the earth was churned up and rock piles were strewn across the land. Abandoned vehicles and mining equipment rusted away in grotesque shapes. I sat in the midst of this wasteland and reflected on the attitude it represented. For much of our history, we assumed that the resources of our continent were boundless. With virtually no regulation, we exploited, exhausted, and moved on. Only in the latter twentieth century did we begin to modestly temper our behavior with concerns for its effect on the environment.

For less than 150 years, we have been using oil from the ground, and in that time we have found numerous wonderful uses for this extraordinary resource. Once an exporter of oil, we now import over sixty percent of our needs. There are widely differing estimates of the world's remaining reserves, but there is no disagreement that oil is a finite resource and that it will become progressively more expensive to find and produce. For a heavy net importer such as the United States, dependence on oil at our current rate has the potential to undermine our standard of living and even our national security. Only a determined long-term commitment to conservation and alternative energy sources can mitigate these grim prospects.

Energy may be the number one challenge in America's future, but it is hardly the only one. Restoring and sustaining a healthy job market is critical if we are to pass on to future generations opportunities even somewhat comparable to those enjoyed by the postwar generations. Economic opportunity, the hallmark of America's past, has already eroded and may not be the hallmark of our future. It is not enough to simply support the rich and the affluent strata below them. America's backbone has been its middle class, and the dream of most Americans has been to enjoy middle class life. That dream is becoming elusive.

The U.S. dollar was once the envy of the world, a ticket to the good life for Americans at home or abroad. Beginning with deliberate devaluation under President Nixon, followed by defacto devaluations under Presidents Reagan and Bush II, the dollar has lost more than two-thirds of its value against strong European currencies. The dollar rallied under the strong economy of the Clinton years, but from June 2001 to December 2009, it lost 44 percent of its value versus the Euro. The dollar regained some ground in 2010 as our economy recovered, but then began sliding again and its weakness remains a threat to our standard of living. Our public and private indebtedness to foreign governments and creditors makes us vulnerable to a forced devaluation.

The Johnson Administration made a serious attempt to reduce poverty in the 1960s, an attempt that we have since abandoned. In its stead, we have become a nation of growing inequality where the wealth of a small minority has greatly eclipsed the middle class and where a substantial minority remains impoverished. This has produced a situation in which much wealth sits idle while purchasing power is inadequate to support prosperity. Moreover, the size of the underclass fosters alienation and lawlessness that threatens the personal security of the middle class. As long as this situation persists, the goal of a prosperous and civil society will elude us.

Just about everyone agrees that our educational system has not served us well, but there is no consensus on why this is so. Asian and some European countries have exceeded us in producing engineers and scientists.

European countries have been more creative and flexible in preparing young people for life. While America's public schools have done well by some of their students, the urban picture is one of an alarmingly high rate of failure. We have a system designed from the top down, one that serves the interests of everyone but the students. We can only have meaningful change if we redesign it from the bottom up.

Other thorny questions cloud our future. Is there any way to rationalize a health care system that has been made more convoluted with every piecemeal reform? How can we adjust to an ongoing threat of mindless terrorism? Can we contain malicious use of the Internet enough to fully enjoy its remarkable benefits? What role can we play in a new world where our military power is increasingly irrelevant and our economic power is waning? There are no easy answers to such questions, but answers can be found if we step back and take some fresh looks.

This is not a book about politics. Practitioners like to remind us that politics is the art of the possible. With a few exceptions in our history, this mantra has translated into minimalism – policies that are inadequate to promote the long-term welfare of our country. Nor is this a book about ideology. I cannot think of an ideology, political, economic, or religious, that has done anything other than lead its followers astray. This is a book about real possibilities, about how we and our leaders could take control of the future to assure one of peace, independence, and prosperity. It will be obvious that Democrats will find more to agree with than Republicans, but the truth is that neither party has been willing to risk anything on behalf of policies that would achieve a prosperous future for the American people.

Chapter 1

Keys to Our Economic Future

Most Americans do not think about economics in a systematic way, but they have similar concerns about it. Can I get a decent job? Can I hold on to my job? Will my purchasing power steadily increase? Can I support opportunities for my children? Will I be able to retire comfortably?

For three decades after World War II, the answers to those questions were yes for most white people, and were trending to yes for minority citizens. In the three decades or so since, the question marks have gotten ever larger and the answers mixed at best. For a good many Americans, optimism is hard to come by. What is different about these two periods of recent American economic history?

A Tale of Two Eras

First, it must be acknowledged that some degree of change was inevitable. The U.S. emerged from World War II with an enormous and unscathed industrial base, and for many years, the war-torn countries needed our exports. In this mismatch of economic power, the dollar was king and our standard of living benefited. But those countries eventually regained their economic footing. The two most devastated, Germany and Japan, built modern industrial plants and became serious competitors in world trade. The symbolic end of our supremacy came in 1971, when President Nixon cut the dollar loose from gold and its value plummeted by a fourth.

At home, the 1970s saw the postwar baby boom hit the labor market en masse. Moreover, changing cultural attitudes and the rising cost of living brought many women into the workforce. What had been a tight labor market began to loosen, and the bargaining power of both unions and individual workers began to weaken. Employers had been accustomed to competing for workers with wages, benefits, and job stability. Many companies were virtual communities with recreational opportunities for employees and retirees. While this tradition did not change overnight, the seeds of its demise were planted.

The slippage of our economic security and the stagnation of real incomes could have been mitigated, however, if we had not abandoned successful policies. We ended World War II with very high marginal income tax rates – increments of income above certain levels were taxed at higher and higher rates. The upshot of such high marginal tax rates was that the gap between the wealthy and the rest of the population was far less dramatic than it has become in recent decades. Excess wealth and excess income were recycled into the economy in the form of government jobs, contracts, and social benefits. This created purchasing power for low- and moderate-income families. That purchasing power rippled up through the economy, boosting the job market, small business earnings, corporate profits, and investment returns. It was one of the keys to national prosperity. A modest reduction of these tax rates occurred in the early 1960s under President Kennedy, but the sharp reductions came in the 1980s at the urging of President Reagan.

America did not lack for millionaires and multi-millionaires in the postwar era, but their after-tax income matched more closely what they could productively use than would be the case in later decades. Corporate executives earned good salaries and bonuses, but the creative forms of compensation that sent them into the stratosphere were yet to be imagined. In the 1960s, chief executives of large companies earned about thirty-five times what their average employee earned, and the companies did well. By 2000, such executives were earning 400 times that of the average employee, and company performance was erratic. Excessive compensation, severance packages, and golden parachutes drained money from employees, who were subjected to relentless cost cutting.

A second characteristic of the postwar economy was that it was well regulated. Monopolies, such as those in telecommunications, electricity, and gas distribution operated under close government supervision that allowed reasonable rates of return. The transportation industry – trucking, railroads, and airlines – was deemed vital to the national economy and was subject to strict regulations that limited competition but also guaranteed service at reasonable rates. All these companies offered stable employment at good wages because they were unionized and their labor costs were part of the regulatory bargain.

In the rest of the economy, a combination of vigorous antitrust enforcement and state fair trade laws discouraged consolidations and predatory competition. Small towns and cities, and neighborhoods in large cities, were still dominated by independent businesses. Main Street had not yet been replaced by retail mega-chains selling mostly imported goods. American industrial companies prospered without serious import competition, partly due to weak foreign economies and partly to protective trade policies.

This regulated economy was steadily abandoned beginning with airline deregulation in the late 1970s. The new economy was one in which cost-cutting, above all labor costs, was the name of the game. Jack Welch of

General Electric became the poster child of the CEO as SOB. In the name of open competition, transportation, telecommunications, banking, gas distribution, and wholesale electricity were deregulated. What Congress did not deregulate, Republican administrations did so with laxity. With little antitrust enforcement, mergers and acquisitions, invariably accompanied by job losses, became the favorite sport of Wall Street. Unions faded as government ceased to protect them. Corporate and individual income taxes were slashed, starting a trend to huge federal deficits. Trade barriers were negotiated away, opening the door to predatory foreign competition and massive offshoring of American jobs.

For Better or Worse?

The merit of some of these changes can be seriously debated. There is no question that price competition increased: in consumer goods, transportation, telecommunications, and other areas. Under the pressure of this competition, technology made great strides, in both production processes and the options available to consumers. Would this progress have been realized if American industry had remained as regulated and protected as it was after the war? Would AT&T have pushed the cell phone revolution had it not lost its virtual monopoly? Would the needs of national security and space exploration have been enough to jump-start the drive to miniaturization and the unfolding of the Internet? Would we have had the dizzying proliferation of telecommunications gadgets that we take for granted? There is really no way to answer these questions except with ideological conviction.

What we do know is that each wave of deregulation destabilized industries, generated bankruptcies, and disrupted the lives of employees. We know that deregulation opened the door to shady operators who pushed the envelopes of risk and brought costly scandals to banking, investing, utilities, telecommunications, and health care. We know that in telecommunications, much capital was spent on duplicative facilities and much income on mindless advertising. We know that the independent retail businesses of Main Street America largely disappeared. And we know that real incomes of the vast majority of Americans stagnated, leading to a gradual erosion of purchasing power and a greater reliance on debt.

We know also that wealth and national income became increasingly concentrated in the hands of the top five percent, and especially the top one percent, of the population. The phenomenon of growing inequality has been abundantly documented. One of the best summaries is in Robert Kuttner's The Squandering of America.[1] Suffice it to say here that by 2007, the top one percent of households was receiving 23.5 percent of national income, compared to only nine percent in 1977. This trend reflected both the soaring compensation of the executive class and the dampening of opportunity for the lower half of the population.

Tax policy played a major role, beginning with the first Reagan cuts in 1981. The highest marginal tax rate was slashed from 70 percent to 50 percent in 1981 and to 28 percent in 1986. This made multi-million-dollar packages much more attractive than they had been, and the favorable treatment of capital gains ushered in an extensive use of stock options to compensate corporate executives, including illegal backdating of options. Meanwhile, taxes on working America were raised to build

---

[1] Robert Kuttner, *The Squandering of America*. New York, N.Y.: Alfred A. Knopf, 2007.

theoretical surpluses in the Social Security and Medicare Trust Funds. Since many states also raised sales taxes, we arrived at a point where the wealthy paid about the same percentage of their incomes in taxes as everyone else.

The modest reversal of tax policy under President Clinton in 1993 sparked a period of prosperity that tightened the labor market and lifted median real income, but it did not reverse the trend to inequality. Indeed, the robust investment returns of the 1990s made the wealthy all the more so, despite their higher tax rates. With the election of George W. Bush and Republican control of Congress, further tax breaks were given to high income America. Instead of national prosperity, however, Bush presided over a recession, a period of sluggish growth, and a second, devastating recession willed to his successor.

So we had a period when taxes were highly progressive, government played a larger role in the economy, and the country prospered. When we cut taxes, shrunk the role of government, and deregulated much of the economy, we went into a period of persistent high unemployment, stagnant real incomes, and dramatic concentration of wealth. Why was this so? To understand, we must spend some time on basic economics.

The Velocity of Circulation

Economic activity occurs when goods, property, or services are exchanged among people. Economic growth occurs when the total value of such exchanges increases because of population growth, an acceleration in the pace of transactions, and/or a rise in the average value of transactions. Since we have largely abandoned barter and indentured servitude, the pace of economic activity is best represented by the velocity of circulation of money.

Suppose, for example, that I earn $100 by mowing lawns. Within one month, I spend the money on car repairs. Within the next month, the mechanic uses the money to pay the new assistant he has hired. Within the next month, the assistant puts the money down as a deposit on an apartment. The owner spends the $100 getting the place repainted. This pattern continues on a monthly basis, so that in one year the original $100 has generated $1,200 of income.

Now suppose that I was uneasy about my personal cash flow, so I put off repairing my car for three months. The mechanic's business was a little slow, so he held off hiring someone for the next three months. The assistant he eventually hired was behind on a student loan and could not move out of his parents' home for another three months. At this pace, the $100 would generate only $400 of annual income. In such a fashion, micro-economic decisions become macro-economic data. The point is that whatever speeds the return of income to the economy creates employment and whatever slows that return diminishes employment. Note as well that if the net tax rate for all these people were 15 percent, then the first scenario would generate $180 in income taxes while the second would generate only $60.

The Propensity to Consume

The great English economist John Maynard Keynes is often praised and often condemned for his advocacy of countercyclical fiscal policy, but he is less known for his analysis of consumption.[2] During the depths of the Great Depression, he wrestled with the phenomenon of involuntary unemployment and concluded, among other things, that employment depended on a society's

---

[2] J. M. Keynes, *The General Theory of Employment, Interest, and Money*. Amherst. NY: Prometheus Books, 1997.

propensity to consume. That propensity was in turn determined by both objective and subjective factors. Simplifying Keynes' insight, the decisions of individuals to spend money are a function of their ability to spend, their need to spend, and their willingness to spend.

A low-income family does not consider buying a house because they do not have the means to do so. They will, however, spend virtually all their income with little delay, because their basic needs absorb it quickly. They do not waste much time pondering discretionary expenditures. As we move up the income chain, options increase and psychological factors become more important in decisions to save or spend.

For middle-class families, dependability of income is a foremost concern. Much of their income is committed to purposes that have taken on the character of basic needs: mortgage payments, car payments, life insurance, dental care, air conditioning, cell phone service, etc. Until their children are out of college, these families create savings primarily with education planning and automatic contributions to retirement plans. For families in such situations, the security of knowing they can meet these obligations is a critical component of their spending decisions. If a family is apprehensive about this, it will delay or forego purchases that it can live without. Often, do-it-yourself activities will replace transactions that could have created income in the service economy. The cautionary effect of such uncertainty is why middle-class tax cuts have little impact on consumption during recessions.

High-income families have less concern about security, so they are free to use most of their income for discretionary spending. The question is whether they have any immediate need to spend. The higher up the ladder they are perched, the less likely they are to have unfulfilled desires waiting to be satisfied. Moreover, their spending habits run to imported luxury goods and automobiles along with foreign residences and travel, consumption that sends much of the money abroad.

High-income families consume a smaller proportion of their income and are often preoccupied with investment. At some point on the income ladder, the accumulation of wealth becomes an end in itself. Maximizing returns from investment becomes an absorbing challenge. Recognizing this, the so-called supply-side economists have tried to justify tax cuts for the rich by arguing that they increase the level of investment and thus stimulate the economy. There are at least two fallacies to this argument. First, returns on investment are best, and money invested liberally, when the economy is growing and capital is in demand. If the economy is stagnant or shrinking, corporations have excess capacity and little need for capital. Cash accumulates in the accounts of both corporations and wealthy individuals, waiting for consumer demand to pick up. Thus, in a weak economy, a tax cut for the rich simply takes more money out of circulation.

The second fallacy stems from the fact that the wealthy invest much of their excess income in speculative rather than productive purposes. An army of brokers, traders, financial advisers, hedge fund managers, dealers, and con artists makes a living off the greed of the wealthy. A great deal of what goes on is buying and selling among a narrow strata of the population: artwork, yachts, penthouses, ski lodges, mansions, etc., always with the expectation of an appreciation in value. There is also the leveraged bet du jour – junk bonds, gold, commodity futures, oil contracts, mortgage-backed securities, and other exotic derivatives flying around among investment banks and hedge funds. And since tax cuts have put the federal government in the red, the wealthy can always get a nice, safe return by loaning their tax cuts back to the Treasury. Of the government debt not held by foreigners, most is held by the richest five percent of the population.

Demand-side Economics

Economics was once almost exclusively an academic discipline. Rarely were its practitioners allowed to speak in public, and their presence in government was more symbolic than meaningful. Somewhere along the line, it became fashionable for corporations, brokerage firms, lobbying groups, and television networks to have their own economists. Like lawyers, they have become ubiquitous, doing their part to reassure the public and help to sell everything.

This army of "business economists" provides a cacophony of advice on investment strategy but sings the same tune on economic theory: less taxation, more market freedom, and the curious proposition that growth comes from the supply side rather than the demand side. Regularly surveyed by news organizations, they generate the monthly "expectations" that are nearly always confounded by the actual data. They relish their chance to appear on camera, their name, title, and affiliation flashing on the screen below them. From these minions, we cannot expect a critical assessment of economic policy and prospects. What is distressing, however, is the extent to which an economic theory once widely viewed as quackery has insinuated itself into the serious economics profession. Even some of the most sober economists accept some of its logic, or should we say illogic. Conservatives know that if a lie is repeated often enough, it becomes confused with truth.

Supply-side economics proved to be a hoax because supply follows demand, not vice-versa. Economic growth ripples up through the economy, it does not trickle down. When George W. Bush sold high-end tax cuts as a way to stimulate the economy, the promised growth in business investment never materialized – it remained below the level he inherited. Before the 2008-09 recession decimated their balance sheets, corporations had amassed mountains of cash but put little of it to work in the U.S. Instead, they enriched the executive class with share-buyback programs, special dividends, and acquisitions. Meanwhile the job market made a tepid recovery before spiraling downward again. Increasing the supply of capital without increasing the purchasing power of labor, as happened during the Bush Administration, is like taking a long walk off a short pier.

Demand-side economics is not a hoax. If a low-income family can save enough to buy an eight-year-old car, the seller can buy a four-year-old one. The seller of that car can buy a new one. If poor people can afford to maintain their cars, the market for auto parts will improve. Manufacturers, distributors, and retailers of auto parts will have increased profits and will hire more workers, who will in turn contribute to the demand for goods and services. The key to prosperity is increased purchasing power at lower income levels, where it quickly begins to percolate up. The consequent acceleration in the circulation of money improves business earnings and attracts both entrepreneurs and capital back into the market.

This was seen clearly during the Clinton Administration. Bill Clinton spent a good deal of his political capital on a modest rollback of the Reagan tax cuts on high-income households and corporations. Together with increases in the minimum wage and earned-income tax credit, his economic policies were mildly redistributive. Cautious as they were, these actions helped boost the economic rebound and create a robust job market that reached into the lower levels of the workforce. Small businesses thrived and the rate of business failures dropped markedly. The expansion of economic opportunity was such that crime rates declined an astonishing 45 percent, along with other measures of social stress such as domestic violence, child abuse, and teenage pregnancy. Ironically, the higher investment returns of the 1990s more than offset the tax increases, and the wealthy became wealthier.

When the labor market was tighter in the U.S., personnel theory centered on the enlightened employer, one who would cultivate a loyal, well-trained workforce as an asset to his business. In recent decades, businessmen have generally preferred a weak labor market. They consider it easier and cheaper to manage workers who are selectively hired and feel insecure about their jobs. This attitude is understandable, but it overlooks the importance of employee purchasing power as the source of business income. The unemployed, underemployed, and insecure employed are not good consumers. A robust labor market may create some headaches for employers, especially independent businessmen, but business overall will benefit from it.

From a macro-economic standpoint, it does not matter if money is spent on new cars, bubble gum, movies, refrigerators, pedicures, cell phones, bridges, advertising, pollution controls, or video games, as long as money is circulating at a healthy rate. The market does a good job of matching supply to the wants of individuals and households. It does a poor job of meeting community needs. We simply cannot neglect the maintenance and improvement of our basic infrastructure, any more than we can neglect national security. Nor can we allow our natural environment to deteriorate, or our public education, fire, and police services to erode. Money circulated by taxation and government spending is both a necessary and efficient component of economic activity. Governments do not hold much in reserve; they recycle revenues quickly.

It is instructive to consider the example of Germany. Except for a period in the 90s when it was absorbing depressed East Germany, it has been the economic strongman of Europe. To achieve labor peace in its postwar recovery, Germany adopted a system of codetermination under which workers shared power with the management of corporations. The federal and state governments also took a greater responsibility for economic infrastructure and public welfare than in the U.S. Total tax revenues, as a percentage of GDP, averaged about eight points higher than in this country. When the great recession hit in 2008, German companies kept most workers employed under a government-subsidized program of shorter work hours. Government revenues did not fall sharply as in the U.S., and in 2009 they were thirteen percentage points of GDP higher than ours. Germany bounced back quickly, and by late 2010, its unemployment rate was 7.5 compared to 9.8 in the U.S.

The Cost of Inequality

We all recognize the social consequences of excess inequality, how it interferes with our desire to live in a civil society. Less understood is how the accumulation of wealth takes money out of circulation and drags down the economy. Both American and world history have demonstrated the stagnation effect of excessive inequality. The backward economies of the third world have almost always exhibited a narrow concentration of wealth amidst widespread poverty, a condition that was often aggravated by colonial occupation.

In the U.S., the moderate redistribution of wealth that emerged from the New Deal underpinned three decades of prosperity broken only by brief recessions. Progressive taxation, along with income-support programs like Social Security and unemployment insurance, kept sufficient purchasing power flowing upward from low- and moderate-income consumers to stimulate investment and entrepreneurship. Government encouragement of higher education and home ownership, along with the leverage of unions and professional associations, helped create a broad middle class with expectations of higher living standards.

Beginning with the Reagan Administration, America saw a retreat from the consensus that had formed around Keynesian principles and the New Deal. The tax cuts of 1981 and 1986, along with excessive military spending, threw the economy out of balance and set in motion an enrichment of America's elite not shared by the rest of the population. Income-support programs were weakened and the minimum wage frozen. As wealth accumulated at the top, the country proceeded from speculative excess to investor panic to recession. The rate of economic growth in the 1980s was the lowest of any decade since the Great Depression. Remarkably, a Republican administration virtually repeated this history at the beginning of the 21st century.

Should We Soak the Rich?

Like Steve Forbes, promoter of the flat tax, or other conservatives who tout a national sales tax, there are many wealthy people who resent paying a higher proportion of their income in taxes than does the rest of the population.

That is true, however, only of the income tax. When Social Security, Medicare, sales, property, and gasoline taxes are included, the rest of us pay just as high a percentage of our income as the wealthy. Low-income households probably pay a higher percentage. (Not to mention state lotteries, which are basically a tax on low-income households for the benefit of the middle class.)

Even the income tax is relatively benign for the wealthy – our top marginal rates are now far below those of Western Europe. According to IRS data, the top 400 tax returns paid only 17 percent in federal income tax in 2007. This compares to 26 percent in 1992, at the end of the Reagan-Bush era and before the Clinton tax increase of 1993! Overall, the contention of conservatives that Americans are heavily taxed is a figment of their imagination. We are near the bottom of all developed countries in taxation as a percentage of national income. Perhaps this is why a majority of Americans tell pollsters they would support a tax increase to address pressing national problems.

We could raise marginal tax rates to pre-1986 levels and the wealthiest five-percent of households would still have plenty left over for their pleasure. Over the past 30 years, they have steadily increased their share of national income and wealth. Some, like Bill Gates and Steve Jobs, have done so by starting companies that became mega-players in the high-tech economy. Others, like Steve Forbes, inherited their fortunes. Most, however, accumulated wealth by joining the club of corporate executives at a time when the restraints on executive compensation were falling away. They have benefited from compliant boards of directors, accounting firms and compensation consultants eager to please, and a novel philosophy that there should be no limits on incentive compensation.

This elite has benefited from an equally curious principle that executives should not be seriously punished if things go badly. Perhaps nothing incenses American workers more than the riches that corporate boards bestow on chief executives when their companies are losing money or barely making any. When a board takes the unusual step of giving the chief his walking papers, they soften the blow with a bewildering severance package of pay and benefits. What applies to the CEO applies in relative terms to other corporate officers. Through thick and thin, they are handsomely rewarded. In the meantime, ordinary employees lose their jobs or make sacrifices to keep them.

At the risk of sounding like a broken record, let us run through some examples of unrestrained corporate largess. None of these, by the way, are cases where executives crossed the thin line and were actually prosecuted for looting their companies. Let us first consider Disney's two Michaels – Eisner and Ovitz. In 1995, Eisner hired his pal Ovitz as president of Disney, then decided after 16 months that Ovitz was a mistake. He sent him packing with $120 million of shareholder money. As a reward for this shrewdness, Disney's board granted Eisner more stock options. In December 1997, he exercised his accumulated options to realize a gain of $565 million. Incidentally, the capital gains tax cut passed that year by the Republican Congress saved Eisner $45 million.

Let us now consider Coca Cola, where the CEO office became a revolving door after the retirement of Robert Goizetta, and which for a number of years Wall Street considered one of the worst-managed companies. It lost market share and its stock price fell from $89 in 1998 to $42 in 2005. One would think that someone besides Coke shareholders and employees would pay for this.

Well, if anyone did, it was not CEO Douglas Daft. For presiding over this fall, Daft was given total compensation of $35 million during his 5 years, including $9 million worth of restricted stock that had not yet vested when he left. Coke had in fact made a practice of waiving the limits on restricted stock, dispensing $135 million in unvested shares to departing executives.

But why pick on Daft? The previous CEO was given a retirement package estimated at $119 million. Coca-Cola's Board insisted its compensation committee was competent and independent enough to make these decisions. The committee was indeed made up of outside directors, but all were top corporate executives and one of the four was Robert Nardelli, CEO of neighboring Home Depot Corporation. Although Home Depot stock had fallen 41 percent in the past five years, Nardelli was paid $28 million in 2004. One could hardly expect him to punish Coke executives for their company's ill fortunes.

This is just one example of how the corporate executive class in America cooperates to enrich each other with complex compensation strategies. Coke is also one of the more active companies in doing business with firms connected to members of its board. Coca-Cola's table of executive compensation has seven columns to represent different forms of remuneration, not including retirement and eventual severance benefits. Stock options were the favorite vehicle in the prosperous 1990s, and when the market cooled, companies began backdating options to assure that they would pay off. They also found other means to keep company officers from falling into poverty. Moreover, much of the money was delivered in ways that avoided taxation as ordinary income.

Let us turn to the largess of media giant Viacom Corporation, which reported a net loss of $17.5 billion in

2004. For that performance, Viacom paid its three top executives a total of $15 million in salary and $46 million in bonuses. It added stock options worth $100 million when they were granted, although the fall in Viacom's stock price may nullify the options. Not to worry, the men will not lack for pocket change. One of them was paid $43 thousand in travel expenses for staying at his own home in Los Angeles.

Hewlett-Packard offers a revealing story of corporate evolution. Following a tradition of its enlightened founders, the company had been considered one of the best places to work, an innovator in progressive personnel practices. One who benefited from this was Carly Fiorina, who became one of the few women to break the glass ceiling to CEO. But Carly had expansive plans for HP, acquisitions for the go-go nineties. When these did not pan out, the board gave Carly her walking papers, sweetened with a severance package of at least $21 million. That is not bad for a five-year run of lost value for HP shareholders.

In her place, the HP board thought they found their man in Mark Hurd, an aggressive cost-cutter with high standards. After several years of enjoying the good life of CEO, however, Hurd provoked a sexual harassment complaint from a former porn actress whom he had engaged for PR assignments. It seems he had falsified expense reports to cover his favors toward her, and the board was aghast. To get rid of the embarrassment, they gave Hurd a package of cash and stock worth $28 million.

These HP bonanzas pale in comparison to that of one James Kilts, however. Kilts was the CEO of Gillette Corporation when he agreed to deliver the company to Procter and Gamble in a merger that cost 6,000 people their jobs. The deal was worth an extra five dollars a share to Gillette stockholders, but to Kilts it was worth some $185 million. Kilts had been at Gillette for four years, and was generally credited with getting the company back on track. He had probably done a good job, but it did not hurt that he took over during the 2001 recession when there was hardly any place to go but up. Despite gains, Gillette stock was still substantially below its level of 1998-99.

Finally, consider the case of Richard A. Grasso. Several years ago, Wall Street was "shocked" to discover that the unassuming little man who presided over bell-ringing ceremonies had retired from his post as Chairman of the New York Stock Exchange with a going-away package of $120 million. The angst from this scandal led to a shakeup of the Board of Directors and a promise of rational compensation policies in the future. It also prompted a lawsuit from New York's Attorney General.

Examples like this could go on and on, we have barely scratched the surface. There is no need to put corporate executives on a pedestal and cater to their desire to avoid paying taxes. High position and high rewards are no guarantee of competence. Many chief executives are excellent, but many are pedestrian and some are capable of spectacular failures that cost their companies dearly. For example, Quaker Oats Company paid $1.7 billion to acquire Snapple Beverage in 1994. After three years of losing hundreds of millions mismanaging the new company, Quaker sold it for $300 million.

The truth is that executives are compensated royally in the U.S. because they control the allocation of resources in corporations. Our system of corporate governance is a sham. Although boards nominally make decisions on executive compensation, the outside members of these boards are mostly executives of other companies who form an elaborate interlocking network. There is a gentlemen's agreement to reward each other liberally and to passively support whatever a CEO wants to do. In recent years, there has been a rise in shareholder discontent over executive compensation, but revolts have not succeeded. The rapid return to big bonuses in financial firms after the government prevented a meltdown in 2008 demonstrates that the executive class will always find ways to reward itself. Executive compensation, like campaign funding, resembles an inflated toy weighted at the bottom – it will bounce up whenever you try to knock it down. The only realistic answer is to tax high incomes more heavily.

Restoring Progressive Taxation

Politicians of both parties accept the fallacy that taxes should not be raised during a recession. Ironically, that is exactly when higher marginal tax rates are needed, to recycle idle cash into the economy. Republicans insist that tax increases at any time will stifle economic growth, and many Democrats are wary of challenging them. If the Democratic Party cannot overcome this fear, it will lose an opportunity to regain its reputation as the party of prosperity. The country will lose an opportunity to get back on a sound economic footing.

Returning the U.S. to long-term prosperity will require a restoration of progressive taxation. At a minimum, the rates of the Clinton years should be restored by simply allowing all the Bush tax cuts to expire. President Obama and the Democrats missed a golden opportunity to get the economy back on track when they agreed in December 2010 to extend the cuts for two more years. It should come as no surprise that the extension given to high-end taxpayers was followed by a springtime of speculation in commodities and crude oil. Gasoline prices soared, soaking up the short-sighted cut in Social Security taxes that Obama had touted. If Democrats repeat this blunder in 2012, there will be little hope of returning to sound economic growth.

In the current partisan environment, refusing to extend any of the Bush cuts is the only leverage President Obama has, and the only option that will both nurture the economy and begin to address the long-term dangers of an outsized national debt. If the political will and wisdom were there, a more effective solution would be a tax reform that returned rates to pre-1986 levels and simplified the taxation of investment income. Together with increased federal spending on infrastructure and energy projects, along with more generous and rational income-support programs, such changes would allow the government to recycle excess wealth into job-creation and purchasing power. The economy would gather momentum, middle-class insecurity would wane, and capital spending would recover.

We should learn the right lesson from Japan's experience. Japan has one of the least progressive tax systems, and in the 1980s excess capital was poured into the stock and real estate markets (including the U.S. markets). Those bubbles burst, and the country went into a long recession. In the late 90s, concerned about its (relatively benign) national debt, the conservative government raised the regressive national sales tax. Consumer demand was stifled, the velocity of money circulation slowed, and Japan fell back into deflation and stagnation. This happened while the national savings rate increased because both households and corporations hoarded cash.

One of the least logical features of our tax code, aggravated by the Bush cuts, is that we tax income earned by money at lower rates than income earned by work. There is no plausible reason for this – it represents simply an exercise of political power by the wealthiest investor class. To make matters worse, preferential treatment is given to dividends and capital gains, while interest is treated as ordinary income. Calculating taxes has become such a convoluted process that many people cannot follow it.

Granted, it may make sense to encourage savings by low- and middle-income families and to make an allowance for senior citizens drawing on past investments. This could be accomplished by first consolidating interest, dividends, and capital gains as investment income. Then the first $5,000 would be tax free, while the next $10,000 would be taxed at a rate of 10 percent. Additional investment income over $15,000 would be taxed as ordinary income.

The steps for doing this on a tax return would actually be rather simple and people with modest investment income would do better under these rules. A couple with $15,000 in investment income would owe $1,000 in taxes on it, instead of the $2,250 to $3,000 under current policy, depending on the type of investment income. On the other hand, couples with $50,000 or more in capital gains and dividends would pay more under this alternative plan. Wealthy investors would pay considerably more. The distinction between long- and short-term gains could be forgotten. To be fair to investors, the current limit on deductions of capital losses should be eliminated.

Corporate taxation has become a national disgrace. Corporate income taxes accounted for more than 20 percent of federal revenue in 1965. Now they have fallen to six percent. Through a combination of rate cuts, special breaks pushed by lobbyists, and aggressive manipulation of global revenues, major companies with substantial profits have reduced their tax burden to a pittance or none at all. According to the Government Accountability Office, the average effective tax rate of U.S. corporations is barely two-thirds of the nominal rate. Moreover, the tax-evasion opportunities vary widely among industries, leaving some, like retail businesses, with little benefit. Closing loopholes has been a favorite topic of timid reformers for years, but the chance of it actually happening is nil.

Since the economic collapse of 2008, corporate America has sung a chorus for further cuts in its tax rates in order to compete in the world market. No one should imagine for a moment that such cuts would be used to create more jobs in the U.S. Having recovered profitability, companies in the S & P 500 Index had a record one trillion dollars of cash on hand in early 2011. They were using some for share buybacks, dividend increases, and acquisitions, but not for capital spending or hiring.

Scrapping the corporate income tax would probably be a good move, simply because enforcing it has become a futile nightmare. We should replace it with a gross revenue tax on all sales made within the U.S. This would be a much simpler and more effective way of collecting taxes from multinational corporations, both American and foreign. To protect small businesses, the first one million of revenues each year should be exempted. To encourage domestic employment, companies should be allowed to deduct the cost of compensation paid to or for American citizens and legal residents. This would give companies an incentive to retain and better treat their employees instead of seeing them primarily as targets for cost-cutting. To some who suggest that such a system would not be fair to low-margin industries, I suggest they look at what high-margin companies have done to evade taxes under current law. As for the appropriate tax rate on gross revenue, it should be set at a level to bring corporate taxes back to at least ten percent of federal revenue.

Keeping Dollars at Home

During the Bush years, Republicans shrugged off the growing national debt, but once back in the opposition, they railed about the recession-driven deficits. Whatever one believes is the acceptable amount that the government can borrow from its own citizens, there is no question that our indebtedness to foreign governments and investors has reached levels that threaten both the value of the dollar and our national security. At the end of 2009, the U.S. Treasury owed $2.7 trillion to foreign governments. American banks, corporations, and other government agencies owed an additional trillion. The bulk of this money was owed to Asian countries – Japan, China, and the oil-producing countries of the Middle East.

We are now in the position of selling off our national assets and holding our breath that the credit keeps coming. Rectifying this situation is complicated by the trade agreements we have signed and the exporting of jobs that those agreements have enabled. Recovering those jobs and reducing the portion of our trade deficit that they represent would be extraordinarily difficult now. Perhaps the best we can do is to stop the bleeding.

There are things Congress and the administration could do to keep more dollars circulating in our own economy and to reduce our vulnerability as the world's biggest debtor nation. The tax reforms prescribed above would cut the federal deficit, perhaps even eliminate it, so that the Treasury could reduce its interest payments to foreign creditors. A serious initiative to develop alternative energy sources, along with sustained conservation requirements, would help stem the outflow of dollars to oil-producing countries.

Finally, a major repatriation of U.S. military forces would reduce the heavy overseas spending that supports them, while actually increasing jobs here at home. Military spending has doubled in real terms since 2000, much of it driven by the wars in Iraq and Afghanistan. Ending those wars would significantly improve our financial position, as well as our political standing in the world. Further important savings could be had by closing many of our overseas bases. Even the president's commission on deficit reduction recommended closing a third of them. That is certainly a reasonable proposal.

Globalization has taken such a toll on the manufacturing sector of our economy that the federal government must assume a greater role in creating demand for domestic goods and services. Since World War II, federal spending has fluctuated between 18 and 22 percent of GDP. Raising it to the high 20s would not only restore a robust job market, it would allow us to make public investments needed for a stable future. Through salaries, contracts, and social benefits, government spending is the surest way to re-inject money into the domestic economy. It is imperative, however, that this be done by raising revenue, not by borrowing. Increased federal investment in infrastructure and energy projects would boost domestic demand and encourage homegrown businesses. There would still be plenty of room for supply and demand in the private market.

Without excluding foreign bidders, we can interpret the World Trade Organization rules, as other members do, to assure that most of the spending stays in this country. For example, companies bidding on projects could estimate the premium they must pay to use American labor and suppliers, and that amount could be discounted from their bid. Another approach would be to require a minimum percentage of American employees on any project. The stakes are too high now to forego any protection of American jobs.

The Critical Importance of Jobs

Unemployment, especially long-term unemployment, is a psychologically devastating condition. For a woman, it can heighten feelings of vulnerability. For a man, it also takes away the socially approved means of demonstrating his manhood. Many men recover from spells of unemployment without lasting harmful effects. But unemployment can also lead to depression, alcoholism, domestic violence, criminal activity, and even vengeance. Unless men play a more constructive role in family life, poverty cannot be significantly reduced. If we want this to happen, male unemployment must be kept to a minimum.

Some degree of unemployment is inevitable because of seasonal layoffs, businesses that fail, industries that decline, and companies that relocate or replace jobs with technology. The important thing is that in a full-employment economy, displaced workers find new jobs within a relatively short time. Unemployment is viewed as a temporary setback, not an ordeal to be survived.

The official unemployment rate is like a rock sticking out of the water. For every worker counted as unemployed, there is one other who has either stopped looking for work or is working part-time while seeking full-time work. Another significant number of people are in the "contingent" workforce of contract and temporary workers created by downsizing. Moreover, lack of employment opportunities is more acute among African-Americans, especially young males. When neighborhoods are characterized by high unemployment, young people may be discouraged from even entering the labor market. The longer they remain outside, the more likely they are to encounter the justice system and the more difficult it will be to get a job.

The gap between the official unemployment rate and the true rate helps explain why the employment increases under the Clinton Administration did not fan the flames of inflation, even when the official rate dropped to 3.8 percent. The official rate had become an unreliable indicator of true capacity in the labor market. It changed very slowly despite robust job growth because the labor market was taking up slack from years of weak employment demand. People were returning to the labor force or converting from part-time to full-time work. Real wages had declined for over a decade, so the economy could easily accommodate the job gains of the 1990s with minimal inflation.

Under Alan Greenspan's leadership, the Federal Reserve emphasized its inflation-fighting role over its responsibility to promote full employment. His successor, Benjamin Bernanke, has been more concerned with stimulating job growth. Given the amount of slack in the labor market, it is hard to imagine labor costs driving inflationary pressures any time in the foreseeable future. The biggest inflation threat comes from imported oil and the vulnerability of the dollar. It underscores our need to address our dependencies on imported oil and foreign creditors.

Returning to and sustaining a full-employment labor market should be the overriding priority of Congress and the White House. The standard political answer to high unemployment has been job-training programs. But as participants know and studies have shown, such programs are little more that a cruel joke. They create expectations but not jobs. Instead, a fourfold approach is needed.

First, government investment in public works should be ratcheted upward significantly. Roads, bridges, water and sewer systems, flood protections, air traffic control, all need attention. Older residential areas desperately need utility wires relocated underground to alleviate the recurring, costly, dispiriting losses of electrical power. Congress could initiate a twenty-year program of grants to local governments to dig the trenches, provided states would require electric, telephone, and cable companies to follow by putting conduits in the trenches.

Secondly, a permanent public service jobs program should be created for the hard-core unemployed: minority youth, parolees, released offenders, and welfare recipients. While such jobs should offer skills and a track record, they should not just be considered transitional to private employment. Participants should have the opportunity to move into regular public employment or remain in federally subsidized work. This not only accomplishes needed work for communities, it is far better than the alternatives of incarceration and recidivism. Thirdly, we should require that some jobs, such as customer service, medical lab testing, and aircraft maintenance, be limited to sites in the United States. American consumers should not have to iron out their problems over the phone to people in foreign countries, nor should they have to entrust their health and safety to foreign operations.

Finally, we need to adopt and enforce a rational immigration policy. Several years ago, Congress was close to enacting a bipartisan plan, before the nonsense of political campaigning made the issue again a political football. President Bush, urged by his business supporters, saw a chance to work out something with Democrats and score some points with Hispanic voters in the process. His conservative base rebelled, however, and the effort failed. Bringing reason to the issue now will not be easy, but it remains one of the few on which congressional Democrats and Republicans might find common ground.

The main points to consider are: (1) most of the undocumented workers here now are going to remain, and they should be brought under the protection of labor legislation, (2) legalization should be done in such a way that employers know whom they are hiring and that they will be prosecuted for going outside the system, and (3) we are in a serious competition for technological superiority, and we should gear our immigration laws to attract top talent.

Having 10 million or so workers outside the regulated labor market allows employers to hold down wages and benefits for all workers, and invites exploitation by the least scrupulous employers. It also hampers law enforcement officials trying to protect minority communities. Moreover, although such workers pay sales taxes, they and their employers do not always pay Social Security and Medicare taxes. Many employers are probably sincere when they claim that they have tried to document the legality of their workers. Putting a system in place to enable reliable documentation should be the primary goal of immigration reform. If it is successful, and if illegal employment is then prosecuted, we do not need special procedures and sanctions governing the path to citizenship. Let us remember that by today's standards, most American families came to this country as illegal immigrants.

Turning Economics on its Head

For three decades, supply side theorists, business economists, cynical Republican politicians, apprehensive

Democratic politicians, and a corporate-dominated media have turned economic policy on its head. With the modest exception of the 1993 Clinton tax increases, just about everything Congress has done has weakened rather than strengthened our economy. It has accepted the shibboleths that prosperity trickles down from the rich, that high progressive tax rates discourage investment and therefore cost us jobs, that taxes should never be raised during an economic slowdown, that raising the minimum wage will depress hiring, that private spending is superior to government spending, and that private sector employment is superior to government employment.

None of these myths is supported by historical experience. They dominated national policy during the Reagan-Bush and second Bush years, with one exception. Military spending was hiked during both periods, without which unemployment would have been worse. The average rate of economic growth during these two periods was 2.7 percent, compared to 3.6 from 1947 to 1980 and 3.9 during the Clinton years. The average unemployment rate under the Reagan-Bush-Bush administrations was 6.4 percent, compared to 5.2 from 1947 to 1980 and 5.2 during the Clinton years. Even business investment, touted by the supply-siders, was weaker during the Reagan-Bush terms. It grew at an annual rate of 2.5 percent, compared to 5.1 percent from 1947 to 1980, and a stunning 10.3 percent during the Clinton Administration. No matter what indicator one chooses – rate of business failures, stock market performance, increases in median income, corporate profitability – the Reagan-Bush-Bush eras look worse. How can anyone defend those policies with a straight face?

Prosperity does not trickle down from the wealthy few, it percolates up from the working many. Investment follows demand and growth, it does not follow tax cuts. Raising marginal tax rates during a slowdown is in fact an effective way to recycle idle cash into the economy. Studies have shown that keeping the minimum wage up with inflation is compatible with a healthy job market. Freezing it under the Reagan and Bush Administrations did not stimulate higher employment.

The quality and security of private sector employment has become very uneven in America. Government employment, on the other hand, is reasonably compensated and more stable, providing a buffer against severe downturns. Private sector spending is a mixture of necessities, utility, and frivolity. A good chunk of the consumer goods dollar goes overseas. Government spending is for infrastructure and vital services, and most of it stays in this country.

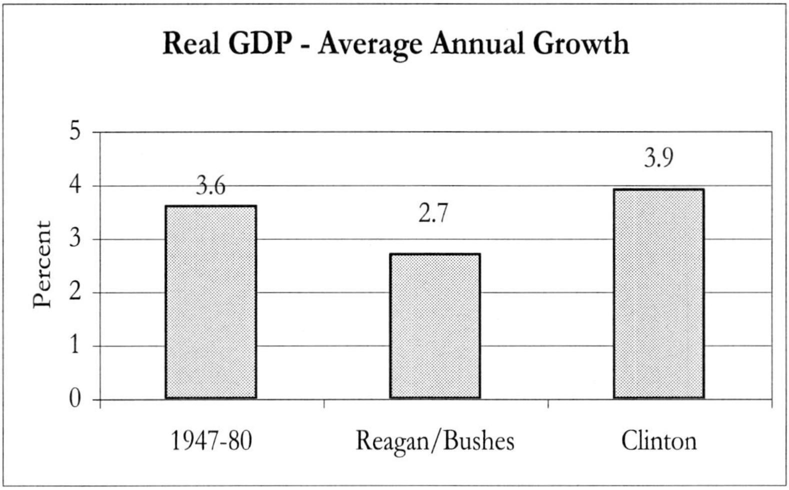

Source: U.S. Bureau of Economic Analysis

Everything in this chapter is anathema to Republican politicians and their benefactors. Democrats, while probably sympathetic in principle, can offer several political excuses for not changing direction. The simple truth is this, however: good economics is good politics. Parties win elections if they deliver prosperity and they lose if they do not. Despite a faltering recovery, President Obama will probably pull out his reelection simply because the Republicans are incapable of nominating a serious opponent. Had the Democrats used budget reconciliation to repeal the Bush tax cuts in 2009, or at the very least allowed them to expire in 2010, the economy would have turned upward sooner and stronger. Both they and the president would have reaped benefits at the ballot box.

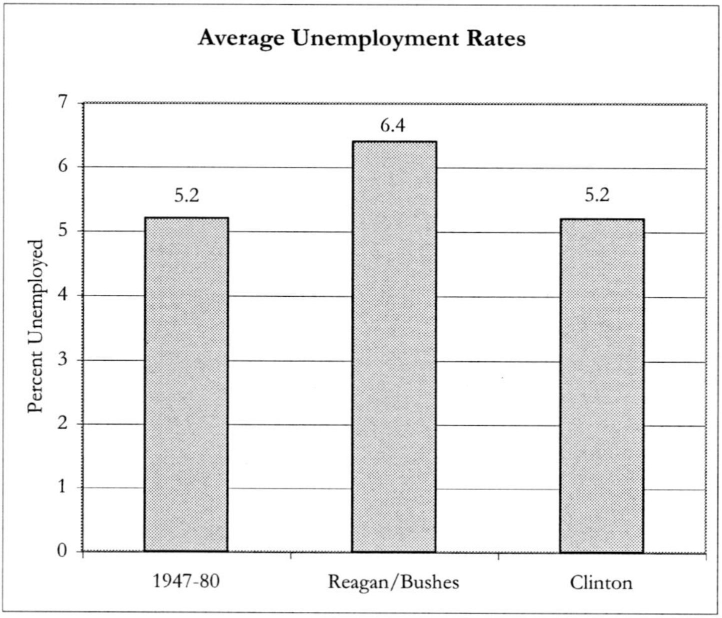

Source: U.S. Bureau of Labor Statistics

The economic policies outlined in this chapter are a formula for sustained prosperity. The policies we have drifted into lead only to recessions and stagnant recoveries. The rich enjoy their tax privileges and the rest of us struggle to run in place. If the Democrats cannot unite around economic and tax policies that get the country back on track, they will sink back to their role of impotent minority.

Deficit Myths

When Senate Democrats declined to use the budget reconciliation process to pass economic and tax legislation in 2009, Republicans concluded correctly that the president and Democratic leaders could be easily bullied. Back in control of the House of Representatives in 2010, they managed to focus media attention on the federal budget deficit and their determination to slash domestic spending. Despite the continuing weakness in the job market, Democrats lowered their voices and let the deficit talk drown out the need for further government stimulation of the economy. Instead, they struck a posture of compromise, one that surely emboldened the hard-charging anti-government forces in the House. With only minority support in the public at large, Republicans had once again defined the context of policy formation.

The relentless growth of the U.S. national debt, aggravated by the severe recession of 2008-10, is rightfully a matter of concern. Heavy government borrowing from abroad continues to drag down the value of the dollar, making our standard of living more precarious. The general fund deficits are even more serious than they appear, because they have been shielded by the surplus revenues in the Social Security and Medicare Trust Funds. These programs are in future jeopardy, not because of their own finances, which could be easily remedied, but because the Treasury may not have the revenues to repay what it has borrowed from the Trust Funds.

Republicans and their chorus of conservative pundits have perpetrated the myths that the deficits are the result of runaway government spending and that they cannot be redressed without cuts in entitlement spending, primarily Social Security and Medicare. These latter two programs, on the contrary, have provided surpluses to cover part of the general fund deficits, and will continue to do so for some time. If Republicans succeed in reneging on the Treasury's obligations to the Trust Funds, the payroll tax surplus would rank as the greatest fraud ever perpetrated on the working people of a nation.

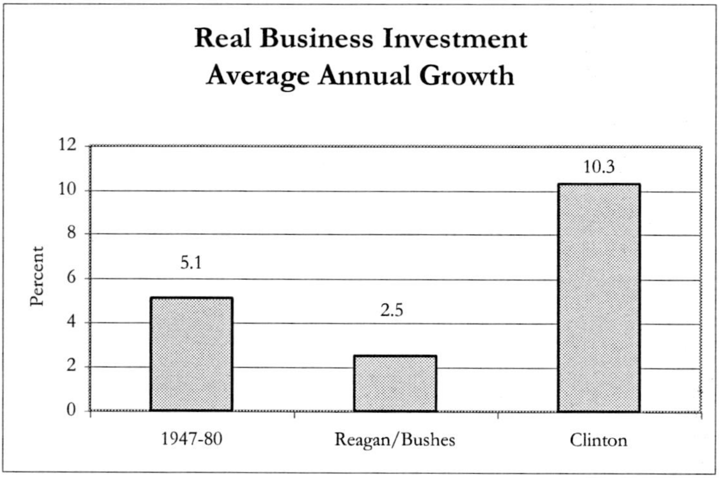

Source: U.S. Bureau of Economic Analysis

As for spending as a cause of deficits, it is instructive to study the graph on page 37. Spending has in fact risen steadily, but no more than long-term economic growth.

Except during recessions, it has hovered close to 20 percent of GDP. Recessions reduce GDP and cause higher spending on income support programs, temporarily pushing federal spending higher as a percentage of GDP. The other increases above a steady line have occurred during three wars – Korea, Vietnam, and Iraq - and during the Reagan defense buildup. Those are actually the only times that defense spending has been a factor in general budget growth; it has otherwise only kept up with inflation.

The truth is that the government does not have a spending problem, it has a revenue problem. Beginning with the Reagan tax cuts of 1981, aggravated by those of 1986 and the Bush cuts, revenue has not kept up with economic growth. The exception occurred in the 1990s, when the Clinton tax increase of 1993 combined with a robust economy to produce a few years of surpluses. It is a tragedy that the Clinton tax structure was not continued. This is not to say that recessions and deficits would have been avoided altogether, but the federal government would have had far more resources to mitigate them and help the states cope. The Obama Administration managed to avoid disaster in 2009, but at the cost of budget deficits no one ever imagined.

The so-called debate over America's deficit problem resembles the story of the blind men trying to describe an elephant. We need to have our eyes open enough to see the big picture and look in the right places. We have sacrificed an enormous amount of revenue to wealthy and corporate America without the compensation of job-creating investment. In this respect we resemble the "sick men" of the Euro Zone: Greece, Ireland, Spain, and Portugal. They too have shielded their elite classes from taxation, and have been saved from default only by grudging bailouts from stronger European countries. We ourselves have been living off the indulgence of the Chinese and Japanese, but for how long? Like the optimist who fell ten stories, at each window bar we shout, "All right so far!" Unless we reverse the policies that have undercut federal revenues, we are headed for an economic train wreck.

The solution to Social Security's own financial problem is to remove the cap on payroll taxes and make the retirement ages 62 through 68. It is also imperative to once again remove the Trust Fund from the general budget and treat it like a true trust fund with genuine assets. As for the general fund deficit, it can only be solved by recycling wealth back into the economy with progressive taxation. This would create jobs and purchasing power directly, and it would boost economic growth, resulting in higher revenues. To pretend that there is some other answer is wishful thinking or, in the case of Republicans, willful deception.

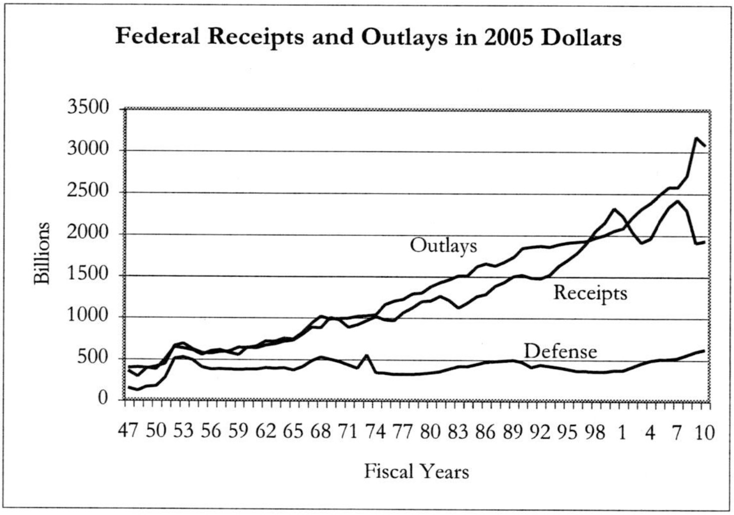

Source: U.S. Office of Management and Budget

Unless we return to a full employment economy, none of the other problems facing us – energy independence, debt management, educational achievement, poverty, maintaining the dollar's value and our influence in the world – will be solvable. When President Obama and Democratic leaders failed to use budget reconciliation to repeal the Bush tax cuts in 2009, they missed a chance to reverse the economic slide before the 2010 election. When they agreed to an extension of those cuts in late 2010, they missed a chance to generate some economic momentum before the 2012 election. By allowing Republicans to push spending cuts to the forefront in 2011, Democrats missed a chance to put the economy on a track to recovery. If Democrats do not emancipate themselves thoroughly from Republican economic myths, they will never be able to stop America's drift away from a prosperous and civil society.

Chapter 2

The Lifeblood

America's first rickety oil well was drilled in Titusville, Pennsylvania, in 1859. A new industry was born, but one that grew slowly for many years. For most of the nineteenth century, the primary use was in oil lamps. The arrival of the automobile began to change that, but as late as the end of World War II, the U.S. produced more oil than it could use. That would quickly change with the pent-up demand and accumulated purchasing power that peacetime turned loose. By 1947, America had already become a net importer of oil.[3]

Since the end of World War II, our consumption of oil has quadrupled. Besides gasoline, diesel fuel, and aviation fuel, we use petroleum in a wide array of products: plastics, chemicals, asphalt, lubricants, waxes, textiles, and others. Petroleum is everywhere; it has become the lifeblood of America. The infrastructure built to find, produce, transport, refine, and supply petroleum to a host of end-users is a monumental system, assembled over decades of experience. We will depend on this system for many decades to come. We cannot ignore this reality.

Much of the debate over the energy future gets hung up on whether there is a silver bullet alternative to oil, a breakthrough technology that will lead us into the future. An example of this posturing was the long-time resistance of U.S. auto companies to electric cars and hybrids on the premise that they were working toward hydrogen fuel cells as the eventual panacea. We have also muddied the waters

---

[3] The fundamental history of the oil industry is Daniel Yergin, *The Prize*. New York: Simon and Schuster, 1991.

by lumping together the issue of oil dependency with those involving natural gas and electricity. We have a steady stream of stories about biofuels, solar energy, wind power, wave power, nuclear energy, oil recycling, landfill methane, waste incineration, liquid petroleum gas, coal liquefaction, and so on. And of course the oil companies promote the idea that we can drill our way out of the problem. It is no wonder that public confusion is widespread. The upshot has been that we have no consensus for sustained reduction of our oil dependency or development of alternative energy. We have a history of stop and start, of dipping our toes in the water.

Solving the riddle of our energy future requires first a recognition of some basic realities. For the foreseeable future, oil will be the backbone of our transportation system, and by the same token, transportation will be the primary consumer of oil. The demand for gasoline, diesel fuel, and aviation fuel is what makes all other petroleum products possible. There are some other important energy issues, but we must first and foremost address the interdependence of oil, transportation, and our way of life. While we must reduce our dependence on oil, it cannot and should not be done abruptly. Conservation and alternatives can gradually reduce our consumption of oil and extend the lifetime of this valuable resource. That is an important goal, and we must also reduce the amount of dollars leaving the country to pay for imported oil. Simultaneously, we must progress steadily toward an eventual alternative source of transportation power.

World proven oil reserves have recently been estimated at between 1.2 and 1.3 trillion barrels, which suggests that the world will run out of oil in maybe 40 or 50 years. Before resorting to panic, however, we should note several things about such estimates. Over the years, they have constantly been revised upward. In 1950, proven reserves were estimated at 100 billion barrels. In 1980, despite all the oil consumed in 30 years, reserves were estimated at 648 billion barrels. By 2000, notwithstanding 20 more years of consumption, proven reserves were pegged at over a trillion barrels. It seems the more oil we use, the more we have.

How can this be so? Of course, new fields are discovered, such as the North Slope of Alaska or the North Sea. More important is the definition of proven reserves: oil that can be produced, transported, and refined profitably at current prices. The amount of such reserves is thus heavily dependent on the market price of oil and the cost of bringing it to market. If oil prices ratchet upward, more oil can be produced profitably and reserve estimates will go up. By the same token, if technology lowers the cost of producing hard-to-get (or hard-to-refine) oil, that oil can be added to reserves. Even then, uncertainty persists. The U.S. has a big stake in deep-water drilling in the Gulf of Mexico. Technology appeared to be making possible the tapping of a vast pool of oil when suddenly a rig blew up in April 2010 and created the worst oil spill in U.S. history. The environmental/economic damage that ensued raised the cost calculation for deep water drilling and highlighted the hitherto discounted risks that such drilling entails.

So how much oil is there, really? The U.S. Geological Survey puts "recoverable" reserves at more than twice proven reserves, suggesting 100 years of oil. But even that estimate may be conservative. Technology is already bringing production from Canadian tar sands within the realm of profitability. With the crude price back over $80 in 2010, companies from Europe and Asia were anxious to invest in this potentially vast resource. Venezuela, and probably more of South America, contains large deposits of "heavy" high-sulfur oil that is more expensive to refine. It has not been included in most estimates. The continental U.S. contains large amounts of oil and gas in "tight" formations that require high-pressure fracturing to produce an adequate flow of oil. They were economical when prices spiked in the 1970s, but have often been neglected since. Recently, renewed attention to these deposits has raised environmental concerns that must be resolved. Finally, long-produced conventional fields where pressure has dropped can reopen wells if the price is right.

No one knows how long the world will have the oil it wants. Cassandras and Pollyannas throw around wildly diverging estimates for political reasons. The industry, including governments that control many of the reserves, will seek and produce recoverable oil as long as people are willing to pay the necessary price. What is clear, however, is that the supply of oil is not inexhaustible and that the low-hanging fruit is being used up. Despite occasional spikes, real oil prices remained low until the 21st century. Now, through a combination of emerging market demand, political instability, and higher development costs, real prices are finding a new baseline around which to fluctuate. There is no reason to believe that cheap oil will return in the future. On the contrary, Americans are likely to see gradually increasing prices throughout the century.

What, then, should our energy policy be? Many economists believe that it should be market-determined. As the cost of oil and natural gas rises, people will increasingly make more fuel-efficient choices in their purchase of vehicles and major appliances. They will become more energy-conscious in their management of homes and buildings. They will invest in alternatives to oil. In short, demand will adjust to supply for an optimum exploitation of the resource.

To some extent, this process will work, but it will be a clumsy process and much time will be lost. The oil market has never been stable and predictable. Even with a long-term trend of higher oil prices, there will be significant fluctuations, as there has always been. The spring of 2011 saw another round of speculation driven by unrest in the Arab World, with gasoline prices spiking to $4.00 a gallon. It is hard to think of a market with more price volatility than that for oil. Supply and demand seek equilibrium, but they overshoot each other with regularity.

There are several effects of this volatility. Investment in higher-cost production waxes and wanes, subjecting regional economies to boom and bust cycles that are very disruptive. The older fields of Texas and the tight formation areas up through the Rocky Mountain States flourished when OPEC drove up prices in the 1970s. When prices collapsed after 1980, these areas suffered decade-long recessions. Many of the savings-and-loan company failures that cost the federal government dearly were in these regions. Investors who were burned by the downturn vowed never to take such risks again.

Consumers were shocked by the spikes in gasoline prices and the shortages that occurred in the 1970s. They and the government both demanded that auto companies produce more fuel-efficient vehicles. American companies struggled to comply, and to compete with Japanese companies that had a head start from their home market. Then the drop in demand for oil, along with new fields coming on line, undercut prices and soon gasoline was cheap again. The auto companies were stuck with downsized fleets with low profit margins, and consumers were looking at the whole thing as a false alarm. The companies retooled and convinced the public that pickup trucks and sport utility vehicles (SUVs) were cool and affordable. They mobilized public opinion against any further increases in the fuel-efficiency (CAFE) standards. These standards would remain frozen for more than two decades.

Oil prices spiked again in 2006, driven partly by demand in China and partly by speculation. Consumers shunned their beloved SUVs, which piled up on dealers' lots. CAFE standards were raised modestly. Again, American companies were caught unprepared and struggled to cope. And again, oil prices collapsed as the world tumbled into recession in 2008. The oil market would recover in 2010, sending gasoline prices back up forty percent. They stabilized for a while, only to spike again in early 2011. The market for SUVs, which had picked up and was again generating the bulk of auto company profits, collapsed anew.

In the wake of such confusion, neither consumers nor auto companies are sure how to make decisions that they must live with for years to come. Morever, it is difficult to build a political consensus around a long-term strategy for rational energy use, yet a long-term strategy is precisely what is needed. For the United States, there are two overriding concerns. First, we want the benefits of oil to be available to as many generations as possible. Second, we cannot sustain our standard of living or even our national security unless we progressively reduce the outflow of dollars to oil-producing countries.

The United States has become the largest debtor nation in the world. From 2000 until the recession of 2008, we borrowed more than $700 billion a year to purchase goods and services from abroad. Oil is only a part of this, but it is a big part. So far, foreign governments and businesses have been willing to hold much of this debt in liquid assets, especially U.S. Government securities. But they are increasingly buying

American companies and real estate. The simple truth is that we are gradually selling our country to buy oil.

Guaranteeing an energy future is an overriding national priority requiring substantial commitment by the federal government. It cannot be left to the private marketplace. Private companies, as stewards of their shareholders' capital, must be able to expect a return on investment within a reasonable time frame. They cannot commit much capital to projects that may or may not be profitable in ten or twelve years. The oil companies use conservative pricing assumptions in planning their exploration and development projects. As such, they can be reasonably assured of an adequate return on oil, but will make only token commitments to alternatives.

Alternatives to fossil fuels have not assumed a significant role in the U.S. because there has not been a steadily increasing demand that would attract significant commercial investment. We have gone through cycles of enthusiasm and indifference. We have funded research off and on, but done little or nothing to take the next step. Given the fickle nature of the oil and gas market, we will not have sufficient demand for alternatives in the foreseeable future unless the government creates or requires it. Unfortunately, the one area where this has been done, corn-based ethanol, has been driven more by special interests than the public interest.

Hovering over the debate on a national energy policy is the concern about global warming. There is no doubt that the average temperatures of the oceans and land surface are warming – the data is quite clear. It is also well documented that the presence of carbon dioxide in our atmosphere has been steadily increasing. Whether this is a cause and effect relationship or whether warming is a natural phenomenon comparable to historic climate changes is the subject of passionate debate, although there is virtual consensus among scientists that emissions are causing it. In any event, this debate should not distract us from the imperatives for the United States. We must gradually but steadily reduce our consumption of oil for the sake of preserving its long-term availability as well as restoring our economic security and preserving the value of the dollar. The government must play a major role, and every year that passes without a viable strategy is a nail in the coffin.

The strategy must begin with conservation. As with alternative energy development, market-based conservation is not reliable. The enactment of CAFE standards in 1975 required auto companies to reach an average efficiency of 27.5 miles per gallon for all passenger cars sold in a given year. It was a singularly successful initiative that reduced oil imports by 2 million barrels a day. However, when oil prices collapsed in the 1980s, the momentum for further conservation was lost. Moreover, farm state representatives had achieved an exemption for light trucks, and this became the loophole that allowed the mass marketing of SUVs and pickups. By 2005, net imports of crude oil and petroleum products had reached 12.5 million barrels a day, three times the level of 1982 and 60 percent of our total consumption.

Congress has recently passed some modest increases in the CAFE standards, including a standard for light trucks. The Obama Administration went further, using the Environmental Protection Agency's authority to regulate emissions. Its targets are ambitious, and the auto industry is using all the old arguments to fight against them. Whether some compromise is struck or not, the important thing is that steady progress is made toward serious conservation. Companies can only afford to improve their fleet efficiency if their competitors are required to do likewise. As the post-1980 experience demonstrated, gasoline price fluctuation confuses consumers and raises the appeal of other features over fuel economy. The higher national interest of securing an energy future requires that gradually improving vehicle fuel economy be the highest priority. It must be the cornerstone of our national energy policy.

Besides requiring higher efficiency, the government can help to create a growing market for the most efficient vehicles. Congress has done this modestly with tax credits for hybrid gas-electric and other high-mileage cars. What would help more, however, is systematic purchasing of efficient or alternative vehicles for government fleets at all levels, including non-combat military vehicles. The Obama Administration has taken steps in this direction. Congress could help with a federal subsidy to state and local governments that would help offset higher up-front costs and make the fuel savings more attractive. This would encourage American companies to develop and produce more hybrid vehicles in particular. Because their range and infrastructure needs are comparable to conventional vehicles, hybrids offer a tremendous opportunity for conservation in both the near and long term. Looking ahead, government fleet purchases may play a role in the commercialization of electric and hydrogen fuel cell cars.

While we conserve and develop alternatives, however, we cannot ignore the possibilities for greater domestic production of oil and gas. The recoverable reserves in tight formations become proven reserves with recent prices and advances in fracturing technology. As with deep water drilling, we must take the environmental risks seriously and pay close attention to operations. The stakes for the country are high enough to justify moving forward with vigorous government monitoring.

Similarly, we should seek ways to increase our use of compressed natural gas as a vehicle fuel. We have abundant reserves of natural gas and need not import it. CNG is cleaner and more efficient that gasoline, but lack of a processing and distribution infrastructure has limited it to some bus and truck fleets. Congress should consider a companion to the CAFE standards under which the major distributors of gasoline and diesel fuel would gradually introduce CNG into their national infrastructure.

There is room in a national energy policy for a combination of strategies, and they can work together on a path to progressively greater control of our energy future. The important thing is that we have effective policies for moving the pieces forward. Government cannot be passive. It must both require and encourage. It must spend more money on research and development and do so with a greater sense of purpose. We are looking back now on more than two decades of lost time. We do not want to do the same twenty years from now.

Electricity

From an energy standpoint, the conservation of oil and finding transportation alternatives are the primary challenges. This does not diminish the importance of addressing the future of electricity. If oil is the lifeblood of our economy, electricity is the nervous system. The challenge is to find ways of generating electricity indefinitely while minimizing the impact on the environment.

This challenge is somewhat different from that of oil. To begin with, except for a modest amount of uranium, we do not import much fuel for generating electricity. We are blessed, or some say cursed, with massive reserves of coal, perhaps as much as 200 years worth. We get half of our electricity from it, the rest coming from nuclear energy, waterpower, natural gas, and a smattering from wind and solar power. Some day we will surely run short of coal, but that day is far away.

The history of coal is marked by efforts to mitigate its effects on public health and worker safety. When I was a boy growing up in a small town, many homes burned coal for heat and the branch railroad still ran some coal-burning steam engines. Our windowsills were covered with soot, and we had to shake it from laundry hung outside. We were breathing that air. That all changed with the spread of natural gas pipelines and the final conversion to diesel locomotives.

Mine conditions did not change so fast. Accidents took a steady toll, as did the insidious black lung, long unrecognized as a disease. At the peak of danger in 1907, 3,242 miners died in accidents. As late as 1960, there were still over 2,000 fatalities a year. This danger has been greatly reduced by the efforts of the mineworkers' union, the government, and the companies, as well as the spread of open-pit mining and a decline in the number of miners. Since 1992, there have been fewer than 50 fatalities in any year. While the incidence of black lung disease declined significantly after 1970, it still affects about 10 percent of miners and has been increasing since 2000. The downside of this trend has been the increase in mountaintop-removal mining with consequent damage to watersheds and wildlife.

The regulation of emissions from coal-burning power plants and other industries got underway seriously with the creation of the Environmental Protection Agency in the early 1970s. Particulates – soot – were the first target, and industry complied fairly readily. Then it was recognized that sulfur dioxide and nitrogen oxide were creating "acid rain" across state boundaries. A considerable political battle followed before utilities agreed to install "scrubbers," flue gas desulfurization equipment. With that issue finally resolved, the long-term role of coal seemed assured. Then came mounting evidence that the earth was warming and that carbon dioxide emissions might be building a greenhouse effect around the planet.

Most scientists subscribe to the greenhouse theory as the cause of global warming, and the EPA has begun the steps necessary to regulate the emission of carbon dioxide from coal-burning plants. There is good reason to believe that major disruptions and upheavals lie ahead if the warming trend continues. If the burning of fossil fuels did bring on this trend, it did so over many decades and has a momentum that cannot realistically be turned around in our lifetimes. We should be devoting serious attention to how climate change is going to affect us and how we can adjust to the changes. The series of weather disasters in 2011 demonstrated that we need major new efforts of disaster prevention and recovery.

Coal is a highly efficient fuel, and one of our goals should be to prolong its availability for future generations. We should gradually reduce our consumption of coal at the same time that we add technology to cut emissions. One way to do this is to use alternatives such as solar energy and biofuels to preheat water at coal-burning plants. This has the advantage of conserving coal to meet daily and seasonal fluctuating demand with a reliable supply of electricity to the grid, something that is a challenge when incorporating the output of wind farms or solar cell facilities. At the same time, we could encourage communities to assume some of their baseline generation with waste incineration, a proven approach used in Europe. Just as we used federal grants to build community sewage treatment plants, we should use grants to facilitate the building of electric generating plants from waste materials.

The day may come when solar technology is so advanced that it can supply a major portion of our electricity needs. That day is still far off, but certainly we must progress toward an eventual solution that does not rely on fossil fuels. Government funding of solar research has been erratic and inadequate. There must be a steady commitment. There must also be a willingness to install solar cells on public and military buildings in order to cultivate a homegrown solar industry. Allowing others to develop the industry and importing their products is as foolish as importing most of our oil. Once a commitment is made to a dependably growing market, American ingenuity will find ways to make greater use of the technology.

Nuclear energy appeared to be making a comeback as an electricity option with new reactor designs and the possibility of recycling spent fuel rods. This may have come to a screaming halt with the tsunami that overwhelmed a Japanese nuclear plant in 2011, causing major environmental and economic disruptions. A relatively minor accident in Pennsylvania in 1978 caused a thirty-year hiatus in commitments to new plants in the U.S. The latest disaster has already led Germany to plan a phase-out of its nuclear generating industry. The potential liability is simply too much for American utility companies to assume, and there is scant likelihood of the federal government taking it on. Some reactors may be replaced at existing plants, but no community is going to tolerate a new siting after the Japanese experience.

Conservation is a key part of the electricity story, just as it is with oil. The brutally hot summer of 2010 showed, however, how difficult this could be. Electricity demand soared as air conditioning systems worked overtime. Significant progress has been made in the efficiency of major appliances, although this has been offset somewhat by the incredible proliferation of computers and the intensity of their use. The public is less attuned to the long-range issues involving electricity, so altering behavior is more problematic. Awareness is needed, but leaders must be careful not to appear to be crying wolf.

Perhaps the most critical component of a future energy policy, for both resource conservation and environmental sensitivity, is the control of population growth. No issue is more important to the future of humanity nor more ignored by its political leaders. Two major institutions, the Catholic Church and the American Republican Party, have absolutely shameful records, but many others have passed on the opportunity to lead the way. Only the Japanese and Chinese, earlier big offenders, have shown a real appreciation of the need for a decisive response.

The numbers are startling. The United States has exceeded 300 million, and is projected to add another 100 million in the next 30 years. It is hard to imagine any conservation measures bringing about a reduction in fuel use under this kind of population pressure. The U.S. is, of course, a small part of the problem. World population has grown from 3 billion in 1960 to nearly 7 billion today. The good news is that the rate of growth has been slowing. The bad news is that even so, more than 2 billion people will be added in the next 35 years. Much of this growth will occur in areas where per capita use of energy has been low, but is growing fast. India, for example, has already added 150 million people in the 21st century. By 2030, it is projected to have over 1.5 billion people and to have passed China. Its small but suspicious neighbor, Pakistan, is growing 1.6 percent a year.

Considering the strain on energy resources that is already occurring, these projections are recipes for disaster. We should be reducing both the world and U.S. populations, not adding to them. Some economists believe population growth is needed for economic growth. They point to low birth rates and low economic growth rates in Europe as evidence, but they are missing the point. Prosperity is a gradually increasing standard of living, and a country can have it without having absolute economic growth. It may have relative growth, an increasing pace of transactions among a declining population. Europe has always been a densely populated continent, and it needed to control population growth to assure its own resource future.

Those who frustrate the use of contraception and oppose a woman's freedom of choice are jeopardizing the future well being of the human race. Those who know better but fear to act or speak out are enabling those who are shortsighted and backward. Every country, starting with the U.S., needs policies, services, and moral pressure to limit families to two children. Religious leaders who oppose family planning should be rebuked, not humored. We need to get serious about this. The clock is ticking.

Expanding the Concept of National Security

Beginning with World War II and continuing into the Cold War and the War on Terrorism, we have taken the position in this country that some things are critical to national security and should be shielded from litigation. Certainly there have been abuses, especially after the 9/11 attacks. But the principle has to be acknowledged – a nation does have to protect its vital interests. It is time to apply this principle to our energy future.

No matter what type of project we undertake to solve the fossil fuels conundrum, whether it involves producing more fuel or finding alternatives, there will be people who oppose it and will use the legal process to entangle it. A sensible approach to this dilemma would be to grant the president the authority to designate a project as vital to national energy security. Opponents would then have one year to register their concerns, after which the president would submit his final recommendation to the Congress. His decision would prevail unless a majority in each house voted against it. Once designated, a project could not be challenged in the courts. This process would provide reasonable safeguards against a gratuitous use of the authority, as has sometimes happened with national security.

In for the Long Haul

There is no easy, short-term answer to the energy dilemma. Regardless of what one believes about global warming or world oil reserves, weaning ourselves from fossil fuels will be a long and slow process. Given our enormous dependence on the current infrastructure that satisfies our energy needs, we should alter it only gradually and preserve our access to oil, coal, and natural gas for as long as possible. What we should not do is continue to drift without a long-term strategy. Conservation and steady development of alternatives should be settled policy, not subjects for debate. In the case of oil, there is some urgency to reduce the currency drain that imports extract from our economy. We must not let price fluctuations distract us from this imperative.

The American public can get behind a long-term strategy, provided they are given more clarity about our national situation. The president needs to be the chief articulator, sorting out the issues so that people can grasp them. It is time to stop submitting energy bills to Congress and letting them languish there without public involvement. Assuring our energy future is an overriding national goal, and mobilizing public opinion behind it should be a presidential priority.

Chapter 3

Putting Students First

I have never met anyone who did not speak about his or her high school with a certain degree of nostalgic pride. Granted, this is not a scientific sample. Most of these people are middle–aged or older, though I suspect that twenty-somethings would express similar sentiments. Myself, I grew up in a small town and attended a small school. It would not have fared very well in today's pressure cooker of standard testing and sanctions. I was valedictorian, but I found myself woefully ill-prepared for my first year of college. Still, many of my classmates went on to successful careers: a scientist, an airline pilot, a graphic artist, a businessperson, several teachers, and so on. I think our educational experience was more about who we were than about our test scores.

Community social life in our town revolved around the school: ball games, band concerts, senior play, PTA events, dances. The students were almost celebrities, and rarely did anyone drop out or fail to graduate. I know this is a far cry from the urban schools that many young people attend today, but there are still some instructive observations to consider. First, we have come to expect too much of public schools and too little of what young people can do for themselves. Secondly, we lost somewhere the notion that schools were for students, not for politicians, superintendents, colleges of education, corporate executives, newspapers, or teachers' unions.

Reductio ad Absurdum

Throughout 2010, a prominent story in metropolitan Atlanta centered on allegations that teachers and administrators in some schools had "corrected" standard test answer sheets or otherwise tampered with test results to avoid failing grades for their schools. Conservatives relished the opportunity to castigate the public schools. The Republican governor dismissed the school districts' own investigations and launched one of his own. The city newspaper pursued the story relentlessly in the name of investigative journalism.

No one seemed to grasp the absurdity of a situation in which the performance of third and fourth graders on commercially designed tests could determine the fate of their teachers, principal, and perhaps even their school. Nor did anyone acknowledge that states have been manipulating test data to cope with federal demands for several years. State test results (which have consequences for schools and students) have diverged sharply from the National Assessments of Educational Progress (which do not have consequences). Nor did anyone seem to be aware that many charter schools (the current darlings of the school choice movement) were rigging their test scores by weeding out low-performing students and sending them back to traditional public schools.

The Attack on Public Schools

With the possible exception of poverty, no issue has been the subject of more shameful exploitation by politicians and the media than public education. Sensing a political constituency among senior citizens, single people, and parents using private schools, conservative Republicans have tapped into the resentment that many of these people feel toward property taxes. Coached by market-obsessed "reformers", they have pushed vouchers, charter schools, and school and teacher accountability for standard test scores. Although parents are generally supportive of their schools and sympathetic toward the teachers, conservative politicians and think tanks have missed few opportunities to trumpet public school failure and belittle the efforts of teachers.

Democrats, for their part, came to believe that they could not get more funding for education unless they went along with the call for more "accountability." No less a veteran legislator than Ted Kennedy fell into the trap. Desperate to salvage federal aid to education, he negotiated what he thought was a compromise with President George W. Bush. The No Child Left Behind Act would require extensive testing for both school evaluation and student advancement. In return, federal funding would increase and more resources would be provided to the schools most in need.

Bush got exactly what he wanted – the opportunity to tout "No Child Left Behind" on every occasion but only a moral obligation to support more funding for schools. Backed by a Republican Congress and confronted by budget deficits of his own making, he conveniently retreated from his moral obligation. Schools went on a diet of rigorous testing but got little in return. The struggling ones were set up for failure.

Diane Ravitch is a noted educational historian who became a key figure in the Bush Education Department. She bought into the whole philosophy that schools should compete with each other and that those that did not measure up should be closed or should undergo a housecleaning. But Ravitch was different in one important respect from the corporate types and conservative economists who were pushing their panaceas on the public schools. She was a genuine scholar, and scholars have a hard time ignoring evidence. Ravitch took a long look at the evidence after several years of the "No Child" act and changed her mind. She realized that "accountability" testing was demoralizing urban school districts and forcing all schools to narrow and ritualize their teaching at the expense of history, art, music, literature, physical education, and other things that young people should experience. She saw that the supposed help that the act promised was having minimal effect and that the whole thing was primarily benefiting private testing and tutoring companies.

In 2010, Ravitch went public with a book that is a remarkably thorough and balanced history of the various panaceas that have been inflicted on school districts, often with heavy-handed disruption.[4] These "reform" episodes have made celebrity superintendents and boosted political campaigns, but none of them has really improved results in our schools, especially those serving poor populations. The No Child Left Behind Act, which was the culmination of market-style accountability, forced schools to concentrate on multiple-choice testing skills in math and reading while downgrading their efforts in all other areas. The many young people who do not thrive in this narrow mold have become "problems" for their schools. Their talents have been devalued. The act ought to be retitled, "More Children Left Behind."

I have always been a slow reader, so I might have made a mediocre score on today's time-sensitive comprehension tests. I am, however, a meticulous and critical reader, and that has served me well in my professional career. We do not teach meticulous and critical reading. Even more important for me has been writing, a skill that is barely taught at all. As for courses I took in high school, the most valuable was typing, far and

---

[4] Diane Ravitch, *The Death and Life of the Great American School System. How Testing and Choice are Undermining Education.* New York: Basic Books, 2010.

away. I did not realize this until the personal computer revolution struck. If there is any skill that should be mastered by every high school student, it is typing.

What Really Ails American Education?

American public education is in some ways the victim of Thomas Jefferson's noble vision. Jefferson believed that democracy could not survive without an educated citizenry, people who could apply reason to their choices of public officials and policy. He championed free public education and went on to found the University of Virginia. Later, through passage of the Fourteenth Amendment and Supreme Court interpretation of its "equal protection" clause, the public schools of America were charged with the obligation to provide an equal, integrated education to all children, regardless of race, gender, nationality, or disability. American schools have been struggling to meet this obligation for decades.

At the heart of that struggle is the American tradition that education through high school should be "one size fits all," with only modest deference to the notion that not all young people are alike. The curriculum is basically designed for academically adept students who aspire to higher education. Although some other electives and alternatives are available, the traditional curriculum is the basis for required testing. It serves as the gatekeeper to a high school diploma, something the business community expects of the school system.

No other country faces the degree of cultural and economic diversity that the U.S. does, yet most countries provide more educational options to match the needs and desires of young people. By most accounts, those educational systems deliver more public satisfaction and generate less controversy than ours does. American schools provide options for high achieving students in the form of advanced-placement courses and some selective-admission schools. Affluent families can seek appropriate options outside the public system. What we lack are reputable schools and programs for young people who are not college-bound. Any attempt to move in this direction risks being labeled anti-democratic or worse. Consequently, we have urban districts with dropout rates approaching fifty percent. Unable to provide a large proportion of young people what they might enjoy and appreciate, we provide them nothing at all.

Our current obsession with mathematics testing is further distorting an already distorted curriculum. Math came easy for me and I got straight As right through calculus. It was a pleasant intellectual exercise that looked good on my transcripts, but little more. I have never used most of it in my professional life, just a little algebra, statistics, and geometry. Even so, that puts me among the maybe ten percent of the population who have ever used any of it at all.

When I went to school, algebra was a high school subject. Today, we are force-feeding it to elementary and middle school students and holding schools responsible for their performance. We are pushing onto fourth-graders math concepts and terminology that are about as useful as the signs of the Zodiac. At the same time, we are graduating plenty of students who have no idea what an adjustable-rate mortgage is, or an amortization table, or the difference between whole life and term insurance, or between stocks, bonds, and CDs, or how to balance a checkbook, or set up a household budget, or file a 1040 EZ tax return, or keep a car maintained, or how a heating and air conditioning system works, or how to rewire a simple outlet. We could go on and on with such examples.

What are schools for if not to prepare young people for life?

Rethinking Federal Aid to Education

The No Child Left Behind Act has been the worst of the federal intrusions on public education because of the straightjacket it forced on school districts. Earlier, court-ordered integration plans drove middle class families out of urban neighborhoods and left urban schools both poorer and populated largely by minorities. The Americans With Disabilities Act has led to ongoing confusion about how to "mainstream" special needs students while still meeting their special needs. It is time to admit that federal dictation of education policy is too dependent on political battles and too insensitive to the real needs of students and parents. Much the same can be said of state politics and state education bureaucracies.

The federal government could best serve school districts by offering support to those who want to reassess the needs of all their students and create alternative paths to a high school diploma. It is time to restore some local ownership of education. What is needed is a process that allows teachers and parents to provide useful input on the curriculum and options available to young people. Standardized testing should be returned to what it was originally intended for – to help teachers and parents identify the areas where individual students need help.

Hopefully, many districts would decide to establish (or expand) technical high schools as alternatives to college preparatory schools. If a district is large enough, it could also maintain a school for creative and performing arts. Of course, all high schools should require some courses in language arts and social studies, but the obsession with mathematics and science could be left to the prep schools. Most people need to master basic arithmetic and some business arithmetic.

Only a slice of the student population has the interest and suitability to become scientists and engineers, and many are already attending private schools. If we are concerned about falling behind in those professions, we should provide adequate scholarships for those who would use them. We did this after Sputnik was launched in 1957. We passed the National Defense Education Act to support graduate students in needed disciplines. We could use a National Economic Security Act today to support the most promising applicants in engineering and science.

If I were designing the alternatives to traditional diplomas, they would include technical schools that would have entrance standards and be treated as legitimate secondary schools. Remedial programs would be available for middle school students who were not accepted on their first attempt to enter a technical school. These schools would have their own campuses, sports teams, colors, and extracurricular activities to create a sense of community and pride. They would recruit instructors with experience in a wide range of skills: mechanical, electrical, construction, information systems, communications, health care, business practices, and so on, but they would also teach what it means to live in a civil society. I firmly believe that, if put in a friendly, stimulating environment where the opportunities to succeed are much more varied, many of the young people who are dropping out of today's schools would stay and graduate.

There is nothing that would help American schools more than for politicians, ideologues, and the media to leave them alone. We need to stop driving teachers away and start valuing the profession as it once was. When I was in school, and during my brief teaching career, the teacher was king (or queen). We lived in awe of teachers, at least until we were smart-aleck seniors. There was never a hint of the micromanagement that weighs on today's teachers. Principals knew their teachers, supported them, and maintained an orderly school.

Most successful people can hearken back to one teacher who left a lasting impression on them, a teacher who was passionate about his or her subject and imparted that passion to the students. Granted, not all of our teachers are stellar. There is room for improvement in teacher education, both initial and ongoing. We put too much emphasis on teacher training and too little on depth of subject matter. We allow dubious, entrepreneurial institutions to prowl the professional development landscape and pass out worthless certifications. We require doses of continuing education but do little to monitor its quality and relevance. We have been too reluctant to use the knowledge and skills of people who have not been part of the traditional teaching profession. If we are to revalue teaching, we should deal with these shortcomings.

Some school districts, most notably New York City, have been using test results to rank teachers, with the goal of making personnel decisions based on the rankings. Newspapers have sued to obtain and publish the rankings. It is hard to imagine a more destructive misuse of standardized testing, encouraged, sadly, by the Obama Administration. The rankings have proved wildly volatile and misleading, with wide margins of error and large fluctuations of individual teacher rankings from year to year. They demonstrate what any teacher knows from experience, that not all classes are created equal. Moreover, good teachers are often assigned the more challenging classes, a guarantee that their test results will not be shining. Any good principal will tell you that he or she has multiple ways of knowing who the best, average, and weakest teachers are. Knowing their teachers, supporting them, and maintaining an orderly school should be the primary responsibilities of principals.

What Do We Want From Our Schools?

In 1960, only 41 percent of the U.S. population over age 25 had a high school diploma, while only 8 percent had a college degree. A high school diploma was a meaningful credential, a door opener to a good job. By 2008, 87 percent had a high school diploma and 30 percent a college degree. A diploma and two dollars could get you a cup of coffee. Failing to get a diploma might carry a stigma, but having one did not mean that much. The decline of the labor market has meant that aspirants need at least a technical college program or a bachelor's degree, and then personal connections or a good deal of luck.

If a high school diploma no longer serves the entree role it once did, why are we so preoccupied with creating an obstacle course to its attainment? We are hurting many students without helping the rest. We are serving the whims of politicians and businessmen at the expense of young people. Dropping out of school is often a first step to dropping out of civil society. We should be pondering what young people need to successfully enter the adult world. We should put human diversity and personal development back into our approach to education, building self-esteem rather than undermining it. We should be building our school system from the bottom up instead of the top down.

This does not mean that we should tolerate disruptive behavior in our schools. In return for making the educational process more varied and student-centered, we should demand and enforce a standard of student conduct. All of the hand-wringing about needing better teachers in inner-city schools ignores the simple fact that most teachers do not want to deal with the social dysfunction that is brought to school. Students and parents should understand that school attendance is a privilege, and administrators should apply that principle consistently. At the same time, there must be a process by which suspended and expelled students can reenter the system. The goal is not to alienate young people, but to convince them to appreciate what is offered to them.

I realize that I am calling for a different philosophy of education from what is traditional in the U.S. It is also contrary to the tack that politicians, especially but not only conservatives, view as politically useful. The question is: are we really interested in helping young people succeed, or do we just want to grind our political axes? Our school system can help us achieve a civil society or it can be one more obstacle to it. What do we want?

Chapter 4

The Bane of Poverty

The United States has the highest poverty rate of any developed country, 2 to 4 times higher. In 2009, amidst the Great Recession, it was 14.3 percent, or 44 million people. We pay a heavy price for it. We spend hundreds of billions, but not nearly enough, on income support programs. We spend $250 billion a year on law enforcement and the justice system, and we have far and away the highest rate of incarceration in the world. We own 75 million handguns and 20 million cans of defensive sprays. We build gated housing complexes, install alarm systems, put grids over windows, and avoid walking at night in many neighborhoods. Not all of this can be blamed on poverty, of course, but the extent of poverty in the U.S. is a major contributing factor.

Lyndon Johnson had a heartfelt sympathy for the poor, and he wanted his War on Poverty to be a hallmark of his legacy. Johnson had a huge legislative majority in 1965 and was able to launch his war on several fronts. Had not the tragedy of Vietnam intervened, we might have had a genuine turning point in the history of poverty. Instead, the Johnson consensus dissipated into a backlash, and this revealed a weakness in liberal thinking about poverty. Public tolerance of income-support programs will be limited as long as they are justified only by compassion. This was seen again in the futile efforts of John Edwards to make poverty an issue in 2004. Our only chance of getting support for an enlightened approach to poverty is to educate the public about the costs, both socially and economically, of leaving nearly a fifth of our population outside the economic tent.

Poverty was not considered a public policy issue before Franklin Roosevelt's election in 1932. It was a subject for charity, the amount of which barely scratched the surface of need. But three years into the Great Depression, the collapse of the labor market was so severe that it brought widespread impoverishment of families. The scenes of bread lines, apple sellers, migrating farmers, and ragged children could no longer be ignored. The federal government began helping beleaguered states with relief efforts, the beginning of federal welfare programs. It set in motion job-creating programs and passed minimum wage legislation. To address the problem of extensive poverty among the elderly, Social Security was created.

Progressive as the New Deal programs were, they served primarily the white working class. Poverty in black America remained largely out of sight in the segregated south or the black neighborhoods of northern cities. The first significant inroads on black poverty, or for that matter on white poverty, came with the bursting job market of World War II. The war accelerated migration from the rural South and Appalachia to northern cities. There was inevitable friction with established residents, but it was muted somewhat by the abundance of wartime jobs. The boom was temporary, however, as the repatriation of 12 million soldiers displaced both blacks and women from the factories. Expectations had been raised that could not be sustained, sowing the seeds of future unrest.

The Breakdown of Urban Economies

Despite the loss of opportunity at the end of the war, urban black neighborhoods did not collapse, nor did other ethnic working class residents abandon their neighborhoods. The U.S. economy recovered much of its prosperity, and it was still an essentially urban economy.

Poverty, though high, declined gradually and was largely ignored as a political issue until Michael Harrington published The Other America in 1962, lifting the veil on both urban and Appalachian poverty.[5] Two years later, Lyndon Johnson and the Democrats won a massive electoral victory, allowing Johnson to launch his War on Poverty.

The War on Poverty was an attempt to preserve social order by finding room for everyone under the American economic tent. By ending discrimination, helping communities organize and people to compete, and supporting poor children, it tried to give everybody a stake in an orderly society. There was even an effort to stem the migration from Appalachia by stimulating economic development in that region. Coinciding with a robust job market in the 1960s, the antipoverty programs contributed to a significant drop in the poverty rate. The maturing of Social Security and the replacement of state programs for the aged, blind, and disabled by Supplemental Security Income (SSI) virtually eliminated poverty among the elderly.

But the War on Poverty came too late to head off the explosions that had been brewing in black urban neighborhoods. Violence had started in New York and Chicago in 1964. The Watts section of Los Angeles burst into flames in August 1965, touching off a riot on Chicago's west side the next day. The following year saw riots in dozens of cities, large and small. If there was any hope of managing this crisis and the ensuing cultural disintegration, the country needed a period of sustained prosperity, a significant commitment of government resources, and patience. What it did not need was the war

---

[5] Michael Harrington, *The Other America*. New York: MacMillan, 1962.

in Vietnam. The escalation that began in 1965 would eventually drain both resources and attention from the urban breakdown.

The riots were both a symptom and a cause of what happened to urban economies beginning in the 1960s. Postwar prosperity had sustained city neighborhoods for a while, but significant changes were afoot. The interstate highway system, the greatest federal public works project ever, played a key role in undermining urban economies. The system reduced the need to locate suppliers close to their customers in the industrial and commercial chain. Companies began to relocate to areas where they could use cheap land and get away from organized labor.

The interstates were originally intended to connect cities and go around them, but under pressure from developers they were extended into the urban cores. Middle-class workers could leave the cities and still commute to downtown jobs. Frightened by racial violence, they did so in droves. In the 1970s alone, Chicago lost 32 percent of its white population, Cleveland 33 percent, and Detroit a stunning 51 percent. Middle-class black families moved into neighborhoods vacated by whites, leaving large areas of concentrated poverty in the inner cities. The industries that had employed the urban working class began to close, beset by both foreign and nonunion competition.

Large sections of cities became nearly devoid of economic opportunities, other than illegal ones. Noted sociologist William Julius Wilson tells of three historically black neighborhoods in south Chicago known collectively as Bronzeville.[6] In 1950, 69 percent of adult and teenage males were employed, many in manufacturing jobs. By

---

[6] William Julius Wilson, *The Political Economy and Urban Racial Tensions*. Memphis: P.K. Seidman Foundation, 1994.

1990, only 37 percent were employed, mostly in low-wage service jobs. For residents of these communities, lack of transportation was a serious obstacle to finding employment, but so was the potential hostility they faced when leaving their own neighborhoods. In recent years, many neighborhoods such as these have been displaced by demolition of housing projects and gentrification. While this has made metropolitan poverty somewhat less concentrated, it has also made the poor even less visible to the general society.

Public support for the Johnson programs was high initially, but by 1970 it began to wane. At the beginning of the 1960s, the public image of poverty was rural children looking hungry and elderly people looking abandoned. By the end of the decade the image was urban ghettos in flames and black families on welfare. Republicans began to seize on the change, led by Ronald Reagan's attacks on "welfare queens" in California. The strategy helped propel Reagan to the presidency, and Democrats wearied of defending programs for a group that hardly voted anyway.

The lower 20 percent of the population began to sustain a long, steady loss of purchasing power. The minimum wage was raised less frequently; and during the Reagan Administration it was not raised at all. From 1968 to 1996, the purchasing power of the minimum wage fell 40 percent. Similarly, the value of welfare benefits and food stamps fell 20 percent from 1972 to 1988. Unemployment was allowed to rise to combat inflation, although there was ample evidence that energy costs, not labor costs, were driving inflation. During the Reagan and first Bush Administrations, unemployment averaged seven percent annually.

The consequence of this was that during the 1980s, the lower 20 percent of households lost five percent of their purchasing power while the upper 20 percent gained 30 percent. The closer a household was to the bottom, the greater its loss. Poor urban neighborhoods spiraled further downward. Without purchasing power in the hands of residents, more businesses left and took job opportunities with them.

As the 1990s progressed and the Clinton tax changes stimulated the economy, poor neighborhoods got some relief. By the latter half of the decade, the job market was robust enough to draw in workers who had been left out. As job opportunities became realistic for poor families, social dysfunction such as domestic violence, child abuse, and teenage pregnancy declined. The Clinton years saw a stunning 45 percent drop in the overall crime rate. The broad prosperity of the 1990s shielded many poor mothers from the potential devastation of a Republican-led welfare reform enacted in 1996. The time limits and work requirements in the law did not have much effect as long as jobs were plentiful.

Unfortunately, the meaningful progress of the Clinton years was reversed with the election of a Republican president and congress in 2000. Misguided economic and tax policy, along with lax enforcement of regulations, allowed a 2001 recession to linger as a weak recovery, until it lapsed into the Great Recession of 2008-2009. The poverty rate climbed from 11.3 percent in 2000 to 14.3 percent in 2009. For children from black families, it went from 31 to 36 percent. The harsh consequences of the 1996 welfare reform were clearly evident. Homelessness soared, and the one safety net program left untouched, Food Stamps, was swamped with applicants.

A Realistic Approach to Poverty

We will never eliminate poverty. There will always be some people who simply cannot function effectively in society, whether from innate disorders, acquired addictions, or traumatic events. Many of these people spend time in prison, which further reduces their chances of supporting themselves or a family. They will always live at the margin, dependent on public and private charity. That said, we should not tolerate the high level of poverty in our country nor suffer its repercussions. It could be significantly reduced by enlightened public policy.

The number one antidote to poverty is a robust job market. People living in poverty face serious obstacles to employment – their level of education and training, their spotty or non-existent work history, the cost of transportation, racial stereotyping, and perhaps a disability. In the late 1990s, employers were so anxious to find workers that they were willing to overlook these obstacles or help overcome them. It was a challenge for employers, one that they would prefer not to have, but the upside was a prosperous, demand-driven economy that benefited them as well as their employees.

The progress of the nineties proved to be fleeting, but a sustained period of full employment would have a cumulative effect on the roots of poverty. Young people would glimpse a different future from the despair that grips poor neighborhoods and would begin to orient themselves toward it. Men would be less likely to leave their families or become a burden on them. To the extent that multiple childbearing is seen as a source of income, its appeal would be diminished by the alternative of employment. On the other hand, if we must endure repeated recessions and weak recoveries, even an improved safety net would not break the cycle.

The path to a healthy job market was laid out in Chapter 1. It requires a renewed recognition of the role that progressive taxation plays as an engine of prosperity.

It also requires a realization that globalization will keep the U.S. job market weak unless the government takes a greater responsibility for domestic demand. Public investment must be ratcheted significantly upward with effective measures to assure that the jobs go to Americans. Both national security and energy policy must be modified to reduce the outflow of dollars from the U.S. economy. These policies would benefit all Americans, and they would help immensely in combating poverty.

Apart from the provision of job opportunities in the general economy, there are policies that would address directly two fundamental problems that perpetuate poverty – the lack of purchasing power to stimulate business in poor neighborhoods and the need for effective family planning. Government can increase purchasing power in poor neighborhoods in at least four ways. It can invest money in the renovation of housing and public facilities, assuring that local residents get a significant portion of the jobs created. It can create public service programs that directly employ residents who would otherwise have great difficulty getting work. It can require that the minimum wage keep pace with inflation. Finally, it can increase income-support benefits and tie them directly to behavior that would counteract the cycle of poverty.

Seventy percent of black children are born to unwed mothers, many of whom are teenagers. Of all teenage births, 85 percent are to poor or low-income teenagers. These figures are an important component of the poverty cycle. Some teenage mothers mature rapidly and become positive forces in their children's lives, but the probabilities are otherwise. Teenage mothers are less likely to marry, less likely to complete school, and more likely to live in poverty. The children of teenage mothers will sometimes escape poverty and achieve success in life. But on average, they are more likely to repeat grades in school, be expelled or suspended, spend time in jail, and become teenage parents themselves.

This country could save a lot of money, avoid a lot of grief, and salvage a lot of young lives if it provided a monthly stipend to poor teenagers in return for avoiding destructive behavior. Each recipient would sign a contract acknowledging that the stipend would end if they were convicted of a crime, joined a gang, dropped out or were expelled from school, or became a parent. Upon graduation from high school, the stipend could continue if the young person attended college or technical training full time. This may sound like a novel idea, but we use plenty of money to purchase behavior in places like Iraq and Afghanistan. Imagine the change this could bring to poor neighborhoods and inner city schools if pursued consistently over a period of time.

At the same time, it is critical to provide confidential contraceptive services to young people in or near their schools. These services can be significantly more effective now that emergency contraception has been approved after years of conservative obstruction. It is time to ignore the pressure against such services by self-serving religious conservatives. Let them find other ways to assure their salvation and let the vast majority of Americans benefit from rational policies.

Concurrently, we need a more effective program of income support for adults. It should facilitate the combination of work with benefits rather than discouraging it. It should include men as beneficiaries such that they are more able and apt to remain with their families. Finally, it should encourage family planning to avoid the role that large families play in perpetuating poverty.

Prior to 1981, a significant number of welfare recipients combined their AFDC benefits with reportable earnings, allowing them to support their families above the poverty line. The Reagan Administration, looking to reduce the welfare rolls, sharply curtailed this practice. The number of working AFDC recipients fell from 14 million to 5 million. According to a General Accounting Office study, most of the mothers cut from the rolls continued working, accepting a lower standard of living for their families. The Food Stamp program is more reasonable in adjusting benefits for earned income, but since the benefit levels are low, there is not much effect. The welfare reform passed in 1996 drew an even sharper line between working and benefits, and was more rigorous in pushing people off the rolls. Once the prosperous 1990s ended, the destructive effects of the reform became clear.

What is needed in the U.S. is a simple, easily understood social insurance that would allow people to participate in the labor force commensurate with their capabilities and personal situations, and still receive enough in benefits to live above the poverty line. Such a system of income security would be similar to one endorsed by President Nixon in 1971. It could be designed to assure that people remained connected to the labor force and that working was always more profitable than not working at all. It could replace the cumbersome, fragmented, and inefficient programs we have now with one that would be perceived as a source of security for those in permanent need or those in transitory need.

Such an income support system should also be designed to reward family planning and discourage multiple childbearing. Oversized families borne to low-income parents are clearly a source of ongoing poverty. To ignore this for the sake of sensitivity or religious beliefs does nobody any good. Family benefits should be limited to two children, and full family planning services should be available free to benefit recipients. While this may seem an invasive policy, it would pay off over time for both the families and taxpayers.

The cumulative effect of this basket of public policies would be to increase and stabilize purchasing power in poor neighborhoods. We could expect a multiplying impact as businesses moved back and added to employment opportunities. Purchasing power flowing outward from such neighborhoods would percolate upward and help boost the wider economy. The logic of such an approach is compelling. Does this mean it would never be tried?

Chapter 5

America in the New World

Before World War II, the United States was not a major player in world politics. True, we had our fling with imperialism launched by the Spanish-American War. We played a limited but decisive role in World War I, providing fresh forces when the combatants were nearly exhausted. We proposed a new order in the aftermath of the war, then abandoned it and retreated behind our oceans. The world that went to war in 1939 was dominated by the British, French, Dutch, Belgian, and Russian empires, all coveted by the Germans and Japanese. Only when the advances in naval and air power seemed to threaten us behind our huge moats did we take the plunge of assuming responsibility for the direction of world developments.

If the conduct of the World War II provided no ringing endorsement of allied military leadership, the industrial support of it revealed the enormous economic capacity of America. In support of their own troops and those of Britain and Russia, Americans produced 300,000 planes, 100,000 tanks, 375,000 artillery pieces, 2.5 million trucks, 93,000 ships, 6 million bombs, and 20 million small arms. When Franklin Roosevelt said we would drown the enemy with materiel, he was not kidding.

From Demobilization to the Cold War

This outpouring of war production signaled the arrival of the U.S. as the major power in the postwar world. With its industrial base undamaged, America's first role was to be a source of food and necessities to the war-torn countries. But Americans did not immediately see themselves as guarantors of peace and security. The overwhelming public reaction to VJ Day was to bring the boys home and start making cars again. The Soviet Union, however, was revealing itself as a troublesome ally, using its occupation forces to manipulate power struggles in Poland and other east European countries. Moreover, it showed no interest in rehabilitating and reuniting Germany.

Soviet intentions became the subject of lively debate within the Truman Administration. People like future Secretary of State Dean Acheson saw evidence that Stalin would try to expand Soviet influence by exploiting areas of instability on a broad front. Others believed Stalin was focused on guaranteeing Russian security against another threat from Western Europe. Former Vice-President Henry Wallace warned of the dangers of an atomic arms race. Truman himself distrusted Stalin and became increasingly impatient with Russian intransigence. When Britain announced it could no longer support the Greek government against local communists, the president responded with the Truman Doctrine, pledging economic and military aid to Greece and Turkey. To arouse support from a wary American public, he used the analogy of a row of dominoes to portray the consequences of these two countries falling to communism.

Truman and the Democrats raised the specter of international communism to secure a reluctant public's acquiescence for re-engagement in Europe. Republicans, however, were the first to see its real potential as a political weapon. Stung by their upset loss in the 1948 election, they were looking for something to distract voters from the economic issues monopolized by the Democrats. They had their opening a year later when Mao Tse-tung completed his defeat of Chiang Kai-shek's Nationalist government in China. The fact that the U.S. had refrained (wisely) from sending troops into the Chinese civil war became for Republicans the "loss" of China, an albatross they would hang around Democrats' necks for years to come.

If the China issue was still peripheral for most Americans in 1949, it came home in 1950 when communist North Korea invaded the South. Armed with a U.N. Security Council resolution, Truman sent forces to repel the invasion, which was accomplished after fierce fighting and a daring amphibious landing at Inchon. Douglas MacArthur, commanding U.N. forces, pursued the retreating North Koreans to the Chinese border, ignoring warnings of Chinese intervention. In the brutal winter of 1950-51, Chinese battalions poured into North Korea and drove U.N. forces back into the South. A bloody stalemate followed for two years, hardening the world into a cold war that threatened to become hot at any time in any place.

Republicans used the Cold War to incite fear in two ways. First, a phalanx led by boisterous Senator Joe McCarthy waved wild charges of communist infiltration at the Truman Administration's Defense and State Departments. When Republicans took the Senate in 1952, McCarthy used his committee chairmanship to investigate and discredit prominent liberals and even average people in all walks of life. The paranoia spread throughout the country, as local groups took up the torch and demanded, among other things, loyalty oaths from teachers, librarians, and local officials. McCarthy himself was censured in 1954 for bizarre scandals involving his staff. He died soon after from alcoholism, but he left America his name. McCarthyism would forever mean demand for conformity and intimidation of dissent.

Led by Secretary of State John Foster Dulles and prodded by the Strategic Air Command, Republicans emphasized the threat of nuclear attack by the Soviet Union. They began building a tremendous stockpile of nuclear weapons and long-range bombers to deliver them. They promoted a broad program of civil defense that had homeowners outfitting fallout shelters in their basements, schoolchildren diving under their desks, and local officials putting up signs to designate bomb shelters. Magazines featured illustrated maps with concentric circles to represent the effects of a hydrogen bomb dropped on various cities. Fear worked for the Republicans for a while, until a recession in the late 1950s turned Americans' attention back to domestic issues.

Stumbling Into Vietnam

The 1960 election was notable for its televised debates between Richard Nixon and John Kennedy, including a nonsensical exchange over the strategic importance of some tiny islands off the coast of China. Despite the public's focus on economic concerns, both candidates touted their credentials as hard-nosed anti-communists. Oddly enough, for all their rhetoric, Republicans had not engaged the Soviets anywhere in the world. Truman had done so in Berlin and Korea, but Eisenhower had passed on the chance to rescue the French position in Indochina and stood by while Soviet forces crushed an uprising in Hungary. Kennedy sensed an opening, and accused the Eisenhower administration of not only allowing a missile gap, but also of being all talk and no action.

Soon after winning the election, Kennedy was appalled to discover that, on the contrary, action was impending. The CIA was planning to put Cuban exiles ashore to start an uprising against Fidel Castro. Moreover, we were about to stumble into a civil war in Laos, Vietnam's neighbor. Kennedy nearly called off the Cuban adventure, only to get a stern warning from CIA Director Allen Dulles about the political consequences of backing out. Instead, Kennedy withheld U.S. air support and the Bay of Pigs landing turned into a comic opera disaster. The humiliation seemed to freeze U.S. policy toward Cuba indefinitely. A wary Kennedy sensed that we were also getting in bed with the wrong people in Laos, and he sent elder statesman Averill Harriman to negotiate a truce.

These events were timely warnings against getting embroiled in the Third World with elites that had little popular support. Much of Asia and Latin America was characterized by extremes of poverty and wealth, and conflict was inevitable. In the 1950s, we had fallen into the pattern of taking the side of wealthy classes against revolutionary movements. The intellectuals in the Kennedy Administration believed they could find a middle ground and build up reform governments that would have popular support. But they had little first-hand knowledge of these countries and they generally underestimated the depth of both economic and ethnic conflicts. This was a feature of American foreign policy that would recur often.

Kennedy loyalists have argued that, had he lived, he would have liquidated our commitment to the beleaguered government of South Vietnam. It was true that Kennedy cared little about Vietnam and thought he could keep it under the political radar. He was getting high marks for the Peace Corps, increased foreign aid, and friendly overtures to neutral countries. It is possible that his success in the Cuban missile crisis and near certain reelection would have given him the freedom to phase out our military involvement in Vietnam. The fact remains, however, that he increased our military presence from 1,000 to 18,000, raising the stakes for American prestige.

Nor did Kennedy feel politically confident enough to change any of the rhetoric that made dissent so difficult. He continued to present his administration as more vigorous in resisting communism abroad.

Lyndon Johnson was genuinely annoyed as he reviewed the Vietnam situation in 1964. He felt he had inherited a black hole that could drag down his administration and reform agenda. But he also felt trapped, given the saber rattling of his opponent, Barry Goldwater. Johnson had to appear firm but not reckless, so he authorized limited bombing of North Vietnam in response to a murky incident in the Gulf of Tonkin. This fateful step opened the door for American military leaders to make their case for escalation, one they would make repeatedly over the next four years. Johnson acceded first with a deployment of 100,000 combat troops, but the number would grow to 500,000.

What followed was an American nightmare. Suffice it to say that the great technical and materiel advantages of U.S. forces could not prevail against the tenacity, patience, and dedication of the Vietcong and North Vietnamese. Unable to find or identify the enemy, American troops lashed out at civilians in frustration. Any hope of winning support from the rural population was undermined by the corruption and incompetence of the South Vietnamese government and army.

Richard Nixon succeeded Johnson and prolonged the war for four years before he and Henry Kissinger negotiated a "peace with honor." That agreement did not last long. The final image from Vietnam was the panic of Saigon residents in 1975 trying to board helicopters leaving the U.S. embassy. We had managed to delay the scene for ten years. The cost: 47,000 Americans dead, 300,000 wounded including many left disabled or traumatized, $200 billion wasted, an army demoralized, two presidents driven from office in disgrace, a Democratic Party divided and seriously weakened, a political system fragmented, a nation detoured from addressing its pressing social problems.

The Politics of War Returns

For many years afterward, it seemed that Americans had learned the lesson of Vietnam: that we cannot use military force to remake the world in our own image. True, Germany and Japan had emerged from our occupation as modern, more or less Democratic countries. But we had totally devastated those countries and terrified their populations into submission. Anything short of that was not going to work. For nearly three decades after Vietnam, the U.S. avoided entangling commitments of military forces in world trouble spots. The biggest operation, the liberation of Kuwait from Iraqi invaders, was a mismatch that we did not follow up by invading Iraq. Then, in the aftermath of the terrorist attack of September 11, 2001, Vietnam was forgotten and war became once again a tool of political competition.

Dick Cheney, Donald Rumsfeld, and the other Neo-cons clustered in the Bush Administration saw the terrorist attack as an opportunity to settle scores with Saddam Hussein and assert American power in the Middle East. Karl Rove, political guru to President Bush, saw it as a golden opportunity to get his patron reelected and increase Republican majorities in Congress. He made the impending "War on Terror" the central issue of the 2002 elections, sending Bush around the country to solicit support for Republican candidates. Defying history, the president's party gained seats in his first off-year election. The politics of war was back.

There was never any evidence that Saddam Hussein had a hand in the 9/11 attacks nor that he had nuclear, chemical, or biological weapons ready to terrorize us with. These assertions were nothing more than a pretext for an invasion that was expected to display American military prowess and George Bush's forte as commander-in-chief. At first, it surely did. American air power devastated Baghdad's infrastructure (a blunder that would haunt us for years) and the U.S. Army rolled over unmotivated Iraqi forces. Bush was able to land on an aircraft carrier to the theme of "Mission Accomplished."

There had been warnings, to be sure. Some military men warned that an occupation force of much greater size would be needed. Senator John Kerry warned about a lack of legitimacy if we went it alone without the United Nations. Rumsfeld dismissed the Cassandras with a wave of his hand. The Iraqi people would be grateful for their "liberation" and would set about building a democratic model for the Muslim world, using oil revenues to assume the financial burden. Not only did we not need more than 130,000 troops, we would bring those home before the next presidential election.

Few people suggested parallels to Vietnam, and no one in the Administration showed any comprehension of that war in which they had not participated. In Vietnam and again in Iraq, we confronted an enemy that moved seamlessly in and out of the civilian population. Unable to distinguish friend from foe, we often lashed out in desperation. An occupying power is rarely seen as benevolent, but if it suppresses lawlessness and lets people go about their business, it can at least achieve acquiescence. We never achieved this in rural Vietnam, and the Tet Offensive in 1968 showed that we could not guarantee security in the cities either. In Iraq, a wave of lawlessness followed our defeat of Hussein, soon degenerating into ethnic violence. We had destroyed many of the basic services, and the violence made it difficult to restore them. A murky insurgency drew support from many in the population who viewed us as insensitive intruders.

The Bush Administration's foray into nation-building with military force was a disaster, one that cost Republicans the presidency and control of Congress. Still, Barack Obama felt obliged, as John Kennedy had many years before, to outbid his Republican opponents in fighting a supposed foreign threat. He castigated the Bush Administration for invading Iraq and neglecting Afghanistan, from which the terrorists had plotted 9/11. Once in office, Obama was confronted by military leaders anxious to use his rhetoric to build up forces in Afghanistan and mount a more robust anti-insurgency campaign. Obama went through an embarrassing period of public soul-searching before partially granting the commanders requests.

The Limits of Our Military Power

Nothing is going as planned in Afghanistan. We have stumbled from one strategic approach to another. We have "secured" areas and then abandoned them. We claim to have killed many of the Taliban and their leaders, but there seem to be plenty more. The people outside the capital are wary of cooperating with us and those inside the capital are loath to take risks. The president we installed in Kabul is increasingly critical of our military operations and hinting that we should leave. His government appears corrupt and ineffective. The echoes of Vietnam are plain for anyone to see. Yet American commanders continue to push for a bigger and longer commitment. Ironically, the domestic political incentive behind Obama's posturing has evaporated. A large majority of Americans have lost interest and want the troops home.

Unfortunately, as in so many of our forays abroad, the credibility of U.S. power is a complicating factor now. We have made many public commitments and involved many Afghans in our drive to transform the country. Getting our troops out requires an alternative definition of success from that of suppressing the Taliban. Some combination of ongoing support for the Afghan government and negotiations among power centers in the country will have to provide cover for removing NATO forces. This strategy should be facilitated somewhat by the killing of Osama bin-Laden.

Afghanistan is a sad country, racked for years by wars of both internal and external making. Much of the population lives in fear of vicious religious fanatics. It is certainly difficult to look away from the abuse of Afghan women and the terrorizing of the rational, modern-minded minority. What we need to recognize, however, is that the world is full of Afghanistans, or some variation of them. We cannot assume responsibility for all of them, nor for that matter for any of them. Change will have to come from within these societies. Before 2011, this seemed years away. Then a curious incident in Tunisia and the stunning power of modern Internet communications touched off popular uprisings in several Arab countries. It will be years before we know the outcome of these events, but what has occurred so far should cause a fundamental rethinking of our role in the world.

The great mistake we make is thinking that our military forces can become peacemakers and agents of modernizing change. Our military forces are trained and equipped to defeat a hostile military force, to do whatever it takes to accomplish that mission. They are not trained to mediate ethnic conflicts or police societies where they do not understand the language and customs. When military forces are inserted into a foreign country, they are viewed as invaders, no matter what their intentions. Competing populations or classes within the country will perceive the foreign forces as potential allies or enemies in the struggle for power, but they will rarely view them as benevolent peacemakers.

Our forces, for their part, are likely to compound the hostility toward them. They will create their own living space, taking what they need of local resources, and establish a living standard superior to much of the local population. Preoccupied with security, both theirs and that of the people they are guarding, they will often be heavy handed in enforcing it. In operations to root out elusive enemies, they will inflict collateral damage that will increasingly alienate the people they are trying to win over. As deployments lengthen and repeat, the soldiers' tolerance of their conditions and patience with their mission will erode. In many ways, the use of military force to resolve ethnic conflicts or transform societies is a recipe for failure.

The Real Source of American Influence

What, then, is the alternative to military force? It begins at home. Long before we projected our military power into the world, America was a beacon of liberty and progress that provided hope and inspiration to those fighting against authoritarian regimes and cultures. Our Declaration of Independence and Constitution, the examples set by presidents such as Jefferson, Lincoln, and Roosevelt, the routine peaceful transfers of power, all made America a model for the world. Of course, we did not live up to all of our ideals. We had to fight a civil war to overcome slavery and preserve our union. We have taken many years to fully acknowledge the self-evident truths in the Declaration. We are challenged now to apply those truths to gay and Muslim citizens. Yet even with the post-9/11 paranoia cultivated by politicians and the media, we remain one of the freest, most tolerant countries. We must realize that this is our most potent source of influence in the world. We enhance it to the extent that we defend our personal freedoms, practice our principles, and take care of our less fortunate.

Close behind our ideals has been the dynamism of our economy. Before the Great Depression, that dynamism came from a largely unfettered capitalism free to exploit the resources of a vast country. True, the federal government protected growing industries with high tariffs, and it underwrote the building of transcontinental railroads. It used its military force to clear away the native population and sometimes to break strikes. But it was not until the Roosevelt Administration that the government took an active role in regulating capitalism and mitigating its natural tendency to concentrate wealth. This was followed by a wartime economy in which the federal government assumed the role of principal planner and consumer of production.

Chapter one described the mixed economy that emerged from the war, in which government, labor, and private enterprise played complementary roles. The arrangement provided 25 years of nearly unbroken prosperity. It began to break down with the election of Ronald Reagan and the signs of future weakness appeared in the 1980s. Still, residual strength remained and was able to blossom during the Clinton Administration.

The Republican mantra that Ronald Reagan won the Cold War is nothing but partisan sloganeering, but there is no question that capitalism as practiced in the U.S. and Western Europe outlasted Marxism as practiced in the Soviet Union. Unfortunately, powerful political forces have pushed us steadily away from the successful policies that made this possible. We have seriously underfunded government's role and forced ourselves to borrow heavily from foreign sources. We have allowed jobs to flee the country and have not replaced them with government-funded employment. The consequent decline in purchasing power, especially for the lower half of the population, has dampened demand and discouraged business investment. Abundant capital in private and corporate hands has not been channeled into job creation. Finally, the near abandonment of regulation in the financial sector led to such a spectacular collapse that only emergency recapitalization by the federal government could stave off a new depression.

The Communist Party of the Soviet Union lost control because it did not move soon enough and fast enough toward a mixed economy. The post-Mao Chinese Communist Party has kept control while moving toward a mixed economy. I cannot explain this paradox, except to note that the Chinese are an extraordinarily clever and disciplined people. In any case, China has rapidly become an economic power capable of challenging the U.S., the European Union, and Russia. In the process, it has become one of our largest creditors, holding vast dollar assets and using them increasingly to buy into American companies. So far, China has tolerated our accumulation of foreign indebtedness, and it certainly does not wish to see a serious devaluation of the dollar. But the fact is that our economic security and standard of living are increasingly dependent on the benevolence of Chinese leaders and businessmen. This is an unhealthy situation that we must mitigate if we are to maintain an economic influence in the world.

We could achieve both an improvement in our balance of payments and a more rational use of our armed forces if we would begin to bring them home from overseas deployments and bases. First, removal of American troops from the Middle East would diminish Muslim hostility toward the West and undercut the appeal of radical Islam. It would give the modernist forces in the region more credibility and allow a gradual transformation of the culture. The remainder of U.S. bases abroad are relics of either World War II or the Cold War. Many of them are resented by the host populations. It is time for a thorough reevaluation of the missions of U.S. military forces abroad and of the facilities needed to support those missions. We could still use our capabilities to support international peacekeeping efforts and respond to natural disasters. We could do this with a reduced footprint and a considerably smaller outflow of dollars. We cannot let the benefits of such a redeployment be lost to the self-aggrandizing claims of the armed services.

Repatriating our troops and reclaiming our economic vitality would allow the American people to do what they do best: disarm the backward forces of the world with the irresistible magnetism of American pop culture. This magnetism was an intriguing phenomenon of the twentieth century. We have never been the source of highbrow culture like classical Greece or nineteenth-century France and Germany. But our pop music, movies, sports, video games, television programs, game shows, jeans, baseball hats, old west lore, and more have struck chords in societies on all continents.

The effect has been insidious and subversive. One could make a plausible case that American rock music played an important part in the destruction of the Iron Curtain. I remember being in Hungary two years after its liberation and turning on a TV set to see a German-language version of the "Wheel of Fortune." Today the "Wheel" is copied in dozens of countries. A recent Oscar-winning film from India was based on its national obsession with "Who Wants to be a Millionaire?" The dictator of North Korea is an aficionado of American movies, while his successor son wanted to host an Eric Clapton concert. Fidel Castro is a baseball fan and Russian premier Vladimir Putin likes to sing American country music. Anyone who doubts the subversive power of American pop culture should note the frantic attempts of Iran to keep it out and the sensitivity of China to what circulates on the Internet.

The infectious appeal of American culture to Muslim youth was undoubtedly a contributing factor in the uprisings that shook the Arab world in 2011. No one knows at this point what the eventual outcome of these movements will be, but they seem to have been spurred by a genuine aspiration for personal freedom and representative government. They have been remarkable in several ways. The discipline of the protesters and their determination to avoid violence earned them enormous admiration. The widespread access to the Internet and its leading networking site was instrumental in organizing the protests and giving them structure. If they succeed in bringing popular government to oppressed people, they will deal a tremendous blow to Al Qaeda and the doctrine of Jihad.

We have spent too many years transferring our wealth abroad and borrowing it back. We have dissipated both our economic and moral standing in the world to the extent that our views no longer receive the respect they once did. We cannot reverse this trend unless we squarely address its root causes: (1) over reliance on military force and over extension of our military presence, (2) absence of a strategy for sustained energy conservation and transition to renewable energy sources, (3) stagnating economic growth, and (4) growing foreign indebtedness caused by the weakening of progressive taxation. These are not the dramatic newsworthy stories that politicians and their gurus love. But these politicos should realize that a majority of Americans are tired of futile wars and snubs by emerging world powers. We want to regain control of our destiny.

We need a foreign policy based first of all on a healthy economy and society at home. We need a realistic understanding of the cultures we interact with, not one based on our own partisan battles. We need to take a long-term view of world cultural change and not try to force it with military adventures. We need to set an example of respect for human rights that others will gradually choose to follow. It is possible that a strong aggressor nation will once again threaten world peace, and we must be prepared to confront such an eventuality. But that is not the likely future, and we can minimize its likelihood by restoring our own economic power.

We should replace some of our combat brigades with disaster-response teams trained to get fast relief to stricken populations and to deal as sensitively as possible with such situations. The United States was once viewed as the good citizen of the world, and it was a key to our prestige and influence. Foreign aid was once considered a vehicle to help underdeveloped countries gradually overcome poverty. Today, much of it supports armament sales or serves as a bribe to keep the peace between Israel and Egypt. A disproportionate amount goes to fight AIDS, when population control would do far more to raise living standards.

All countries, democratic and authoritarian, are susceptible to the lure of using foreign policy as a weapon of domestic political conflict or control. The regimes in Iran, North Korea, and Cuba rely on the threat of foreign enemies to rationalize their suppression. But competing forces in democratic countries find the exaggeration of external threats no less useful, as the Bush Administration has amply demonstrated. There is little hope that Republicans will forego this political strategy, pressed as they are to garner support on economic grounds. Many Democratic leaders possess a more nuanced understanding of other countries and of appropriate strategies for dealing with them, but they have been too easily intimidated by the demagoguery of the right. Unless they find the courage to resist, our foreign policy will continue to be a series of blunders and a failure to realize our potential.

Confronting Terrorism

The 9/11 attacks were horrific and definitely terrifying, and an initial reaction of fear was warranted. It was soon clear, however, that the attacks had to be carried out in close concert with each other in order to succeed. In fact, the fourth attack did not succeed because the plane's passengers had word of the first three. The strategy of hijacking airplanes to use as missiles was quickly thwarted by locking cabin doors and changing the modus operandi for dealing with hijackers. From that point on, President Bush and other opinion leaders had two choices: stoke the fires of paranoia or resist them. Most chose the former.

Destruction of the Taliban regime in Afghanistan and disruption of Al Qaeda's sanctuary was certainly justified, and it was carried out with a remarkably small CIA and special forces operation. This opened, of course, the whole question of what to do with Afghanistan, a question the Bush Administration chose to minimize in favor of its disastrous invasion of Iraq. In truth, the original Afghan operation was probably the apex of what military forces on the ground could accomplish in the fight against terrorism. From that point on, our military presence in Muslim countries served primarily to support Osama bin-Laden's charge that we were waging war against Islam, as well as to heighten the hostility between Sunnis and Shia.

The threat of Islamist terrorism has not gone away, nor will it for some time. Al Qaeda's capacity for large-scale, carefully planned and orchestrated attacks has been greatly diminished, but a new version of the threat has emerged. Muslim citizens of western countries who became seduced by bin-Laden's rhetoric have traveled to Pakistan and received training in the use of homemade explosives. Successful attacks were carried out in Spain and Britain, and several have failed in the U.S. The worst incident in this country was the shootings by a Muslim officer at Fort Hood.

We can diminish the impact of terrorism on American society if we acknowledge three aspects of reality. First, we should recognize that our military presence in Iraq, Afghanistan, and Saudi Arabia is central to the Jihadist appeal and its ability to recruit potential terrorists. These deployments serve no long-term interest of the United States, and there is nothing we could do to make America safer and recover our normalcy than to liquidate them.

Second, the cooperation of the CIA, FBI, and local police forces in ferreting out and suppressing potential terrorist attacks is far more effective than military operations. There have been a number of successes so far that, along with some dumb luck, have kept the homeland nearly free of terrorist casualties since 9/11. (In contrast, tens of thousands of young Americans have been killed or wounded by terrorists in Iraq and Afghanistan. For some reason, we seem to discount these lives when assessing the impact of terrorism.) For intelligence operations to truly succeed, we need the cooperation of Muslim-Americans, the vast majority of whom are anxious to help. Demonizing them, as some politicians and our own religions fanatics are wont to do, is self-defeating.

Third, we have been our own worst enemies in magnifying the cost of the terrorist threat. The original Bush Administration restrictions on airports nearly bankrupted the airline industry. Airline travel has remained distinctly unpleasant ever since, thanks to the government's takeover of airport security. It is hard to quantify the cost of the additional travel time imposed by this security. If not for the advent of wifi communications, it would be monumental. We have imposed mindless security measures at just about every public event, except at political candidate gatherings where security would truly be warranted. New areas of security upgrade are constantly being proposed and hyped by the media. The truth is that the odds of an American civilian being killed by terrorism are so small as to be negligible. We are at far greater risk from disturbed, disgruntled, or alienated individuals with access to guns. We are truly at risk when we climb into our cars or check into a hospital. There are certainly dangers to be wary of in America, but Islamist terrorism is not one of them.

The popular uprisings in Egypt and other Arab countries, especially the conflict in Libya, presented a thorny dilemma for President Obama. Several of the threatened rulers have been, like Saddam Hussein, enemies of Al Qaeda and the Jihadist forces. Yet, indigenous uprisings against autocratic regimes, inspired by our example but not orchestrated by us, are something we should welcome. What are we to do, then, when brutal repression by the tyrant is imminent? Whatever we choose to do can be seen as precedent by both rulers and the modernist middle class movements seeking change. Obama chose reluctantly to intervene in Libya with a measured response endorsed by NATO and the United Nations Security Council. He gambled that an acceptable outcome could be achieved without deeper involvement, as occurred with Kosovo and Serbia in the late 1990s.

One lesson from these events should be clear. Liquidation of our major role in Iraq and Afghanistan would enable us to provide limited strategic support to democratic movements when the situations clearly warrant it, as in Libya. We cannot predict or dictate the outcomes of this ferment, but we can express sympathies consistent with our own traditions and articulate principles that may be useful to nascent groups. We can place ourselves on the right side of history, a place we have not always been but always should be.

Chapter 6

Reforming the Process

Radical as it was for its time, the U.S. constitution is a peculiarly conservative document. The convention that created it was made up largely of businessmen and landowners who feared that state legislatures were falling under the control of populist majorities. Led by Alexander Hamilton, the preponderance of founding fathers wanted a strong federal government to protect property rights and the sanctity of contracts. They designated a number of powers to the Congress, and added the supremacy clause to assure that the constitution and laws passed under it would preempt anything done by the states.

James Madison, a key architect of the new government, was at heart a democrat, but he nonetheless worried about abuse by popular majorities. Hence the convention gave the president a veto power over congressional legislation, his role being viewed more as chief guardian than as chief legislator. Madison also pushed the concept of a bicameral legislature, in which the Senate would be a calm, deliberative body to balance the more volatile House of Representatives. Moreover, Madison secured agreement that amendments would be added to protect individual rights against a potential "tyranny of the majority." These ten amendments, our Bill of Rights, became the defining principles of American democracy. Originally meant as conservative protections, they came to represent the hopes of democratic reformers and revolutionaries around the world.

The first government elected under the new constitution was anything but passive. Hamilton, as

Secretary of the Treasury, achieved the establishment of a national bank and the assumption of state revolutionary war debts. The federal government became the principle source of currency and guarantor of contracts, even resorting to military force in a few circumstances to enforce its authority to tax and regulate commerce. Hamilton and the Federalists, ancestors of the Whigs and Republicans, set the precedent of the federal government as facilitator of economic growth. For many decades, high tariffs were used to protect growing domestic industries. From canals and roads to the railroads, airports, and interstate highway system, the federal government's leadership in building a national transportation network has been a goal of the business community and its political allies. It was only when Franklin Roosevelt used federal power on behalf of the working class that the business community became wary of Washington.

A Few Breakthroughs

The entrepreneurial class may have gotten what it wanted from the federal government, but the cumbersome machinery created in 1787 has frustrated popular opinion in the U.S. At only three times in our history has a legislative agenda been passed that served the majority of Americans. The first was an aberration. The Civil War Amendments, 13, 14, and 15, were passed by a congress that excluded former southern representatives, and ratification by those states was a condition of their readmission to the Union. The amendments were partly inspired by genuine reformers in Congress and partly by the Republicans' desire to enlist newly freed slaves as loyal voters. It is doubtful that anyone at the time envisaged the effect these amendments would have on civil liberties in the twentieth century. With recent lawsuits claiming "reverse discrimination" against white males, it would seem that every group in America has sought relief under the equal protection clause of the Fourteenth Amendment.

An economically prostrate country forsook the Republicans in 1932 and elected massive Democratic majorities to support Franklin Roosevelt's agenda. Over the next five years, the character of national government changed dramatically, as Washington took responsibility for the health of the economy, the viability of collective bargaining, and a minimum level of personal security for the unemployed and elderly. The redistribution of income that started under the New Deal and expanded in wartime became an engine of economic growth that powered our standard of living for several decades.

The final watershed occurred in 1965, in the wake of Barry Goldwater's disastrous presidential campaign to undo the New Deal. Once again, Democratic majorities were so overwhelming that Lyndon Johnson and liberal leaders were able to surmount the roadblocks in the system. Congress enacted Medicare and Medicaid, federal support of public and higher education, protection of voting rights, and a direct assault on the roots of both urban and rural poverty. Had it not been for the tragedy of the Vietnam War, this fertile period might have led to a sustained liberal consensus with further progress on national problems.

On two other occasions, significant pieces of legislation were passed to deal with specific problems. A bipartisan response to the 1973 oil embargo led to passage in 1975 of the corporate average fuel economy (CAFE) standards that helped the country through its first energy crisis. In 1993, a Democratic congress used the budget reconciliation process to barely pass President Clinton's tax increases that reversed soaring budget deficits. The resulting modest redistribution of income propelled several years of prosperity.

Republicans used the budget reconciliation stratagem to pass tax cuts in 2001 and 2003 that turned surpluses into deficits and stalled economic growth. In 2009, the refusal of Democratic Senators to use the same process so delayed and compromised President Obama's agenda that he got no credit for it. Republicans recaptured the House and a golden opportunity to address serious national problems was lost.

A Senate We Could Do Without

The primary culprit in our national policy failures has been the U.S. Senate. Despite the Progressive Era amendment for direct election of senators, it ranks as one of the most unrepresentative bodies in the world. The compromise that gave each state two senators did not seem unreasonable in the world of 1787, but it has become ludicrous in today's world. Thirty states with just 15 percent of the U.S. population have 60 of the 100 seats in the Senate. The four Democratic senators most responsible for letting the president down in 2009 represented just 2.3 percent of the country.

The skewed representation in the Senate is only one of its problems. It labors under archaic rules that reflect nothing but the arrogance of the senators themselves. Cloture motions, which require 60 votes to end debate on a bill, allow a minority to endlessly frustrate the popular will. Other rules allow individual senators to stall both legislation and confirmations of presidential appointees. None of the excuses for these rules are persuasive, or even rational. They exist solely to prevent decisive action by Congress and to inflate the self-importance of members.

If Madison imagined the Senate as a deliberative body, it has rarely been so. Perhaps from the late 1950s to the 1970s, when moderate liberals of both parties cooperated, it functioned as a constructive legislative body. That has long since ceased, and today it is the site of withering partisan combat. The Republican minority brought the business of the Senate to a virtual standstill in 2009-10, preventing even the passage of annual appropriations to fund the government. The Senate of today is serving no national purpose.

The Senate seems incapable of reforming itself unless subjected to significant public pressure. One approach might be a series of advisory referenda in states calling for all Senate votes except on treaties to be decided by simple majority vote. These could be followed up by requesting pledges from Senate candidates similar to the anti-tax pledges used by conservatives. Obviously, such a strategy would require a determined organizational effort, from either new or existing organizations.

For most of our national history, we have muddled through and sometimes thrived with an ineffective national legislature. Our abundance of land and natural resources, the protection of our oceans, the human energy brought by waves of immigration, and the balance of public and private enterprise in our economy were sufficient to propel the nation forward. In times of crisis, especially the Great Depression and the civil unrest of the 1960s, decisive elections produced majorities that could temporarily overcome the obstacles in the system.

We are no longer in that happy circumstance. We face serious challenges in assuring our energy future, restoring economic opportunity, preserving the value of the dollar, mitigating the effects of poverty, and preventing large transfers of our national assets to foreign investors and governments. To be saddled with a dysfunctional national legislature means drifting into a long period of national decline.

Reforming the Senate would certainly be a major step in the right direction, but it would not cure a malady that has steadily encroached on national policy-making for the past thirty years. The Republican Party has been turned into an ideological movement in which there is no room for objective assessment of facts and history. This would be regrettable, but not a tragedy, if the Democratic Party and the national media had resisted this assault on reason and knowledge. Unfortunately, Democrats have been tepid in defense of their own traditions and have allowed their voices to be drowned out by the unrelenting misinformation from the right. The media, for its part, has all but abandoned the notion of objective truth by giving credibility to all assertions, no matter how nonsensical. Some attribute these developments to the pervasive control that Wall Street and corporate America exercise in the entire political and media world. I do not necessarily dispute this, but I blame even more the declining quality of higher education. Somehow, mythology has crowded out the rationality that Jefferson imagined for America.

In Closing

Can America Survive Its Future?

There are two important subjects that I have not treated in detail. I have written about health care before, about the need for an efficient, straightforward national program that would spread risk as broadly as possible. The fragmentation of risk in our current system produces a pervasive game of shifting costs among insurers, providers, consumers, and government. The law passed in 2010, with appalling political agony, left this byzantine system intact and in fact added to the confusion. It seems clear now that the passage of Medicare in 1965 was the high-water mark of sensible health care reform. It is hard to imagine that opportunity will knock again. So I am violating my own rule and leaving the subject to its political fate.

I am also passing on the subject of Internet security, but only because I do not feel competent to examine it. Malicious use of this communications marvel has already been unnerving, but the worst could be yet to come. The apparent disruption of the Iranian nuclear program by the Stuxnet virus is a chilling example of what could happen if governments embark on a cyberwar arms race. We do not know for sure where Stuxnet originated, but signs point to either Israel or the U.S. In a few short decades, modern society has become as dependent on the Internet as on electricity itself. The notion of war being conducted in cyberspace is almost as frightening as nuclear war. Let us hope that defense and deterrence will prevail over offense.

If the twentieth was an American century, the twenty-first is shaping up as an Asian century. We need not begrudge other countries' maturation into economic powers but we should not stand by while they surpass us. We should be rebuilding the foundation that made us prosperous and prominent. That foundation had four pillars: a strong dollar, progressive taxation that tempered inequality and enlarged the middle class, economic regulation that restrained irresponsible behavior, and constitutional guarantees that promoted tolerance of diversity and freedom of speech.

Is there any chance that we can recommit ourselves to these principles? Can we begin to liberate ourselves from imported oil and set a long, patient course toward energy independence? Can we curtail our military ambitions and start bringing our people and dollars home? Can we recognize the public interest in adopting sensible policies to alleviate poverty? Can we bring some common sense back to public education and get the "reformers" out of it? Can we actually start thinking about the future and how we are going to get there?

I wish I could be more optimistic about the answers to these questions. We have one political party that, like the Marxist parties of the last century, has achieved discipline around an ideology that ignores science, denies history, and imagines the present. Most Americans are proud of our parks, highways, airports, clean water and waterways, police, fire, and sanitation services, public schools and libraries, and our economic security programs. They believe it their patriotic duty to support these things. A narrow minority bent on tearing down our government, however, has taken over the Republican Party.

Our other party contains many members who seek objective truth, but the party itself has had great difficulty organizing around substantive change. Its disability in this regard leaves the public bewildered and susceptible to the mantras of the opposition. Too many Democrats have lost touch with their own traditions. They are not building on the legacy of Franklin Roosevelt, or even on those of Lyndon Johnson and Bill Clinton. They are not pursuing policies that have served the country and their party well in the past, and would serve them well in today's world.

When one political party has forfeited all claims to constructive leadership, this is not a time to extol the virtues of political accommodation. In the challenges of the twenty-first century, with our natural advantages diminished, there is less margin for muddling through. Somehow, our system has to generate sustained purpose. If not, we may be seeing the twilight of the world's oldest democracy.